THE TEACHER'S BOOK OF LISTS

OTHER GOODYEAR BOOKS IN GENERAL METHODS & CENTERS

AH HAH! The Inquiry Process of Generating and Testing Knowledge
John McCollum

A CALENDAR OF HOME/SCHOOL ACTIVITIES
Jo Anne Patricia Brosnahan and Barbara Walters Milne

CHANGE FOR CHILDREN Ideas and Activities for Individualizing Learning
Sandra N. Kaplan, Jo Ann B. Kaplan, Sheila K. Madsen, Bette K. Taylor

CREATING A LEARNING ENVIRONMENT A Learning Center Handbook
Ethel Breyfogle, Susan Nelson, Carol Pitts, Pamela Santich

THE LEARNING CENTER BOOK An Integrated Approach
Tom Davidson, Phyllis Fountain, Rachel Grogan, Verl Short, Judy Steely, Katherine Freeman

ONE AT A TIME ALL AT ONCE The Creative Teacher's Guide to Individualized Instruction Without Anarchy
Jack E. Blackburn and W. Conrad Powell

OPEN SESAME A Primer in Open Education
Evelyn M. Carswell and Darrell L. Roubinek

THE OTHER SIDE OF THE REPORT CARD A How-to-Do-It Program for Affective Education
Larry Chase

THE TEACHER'S CHOICE Ideas and Activities for Teaching Basic Skills
Sandra N. Kaplan, Sheila K. Madsen, Bette T. Gould

TEACHING FOR LEARNING Applying Educational Psychology in the Classroom
Myron H. Dembo

OTHER WAYS, OTHER MEANS Altered Awareness Activities for Receptive Learning
Alton Harrison and Diann Musial

WILL THE REAL TEACHER PLEASE STAND UP? A Primer in Humanistic Education, 2nd edition
Mary Greer and Bonnie Rubinstein

A YOUNG CHILD EXPERIENCES Activities for Teaching and Learning
Sandra N. Kaplan, Jo Ann B. Kaplan, Sheila K. Madsen, Bette T. Gould

For information about these, or Goodyear books in Language Arts, Reading, Science, Math, and Social Studies, write to

JANET JACKSON
Goodyear Publishing Company *(213) 393-6731*
1640 Fifth Street
Santa Monica, CA 90401

THE TEACHER'S BOOK OF LISTS

Sheila Madsen and Bette Gould

Goodyear Publishing Company, Inc. • Santa Monica, California

Library of Congress Cataloging in Publication Data

Madsen, Sheila K 1940-
The teacher's book of lists.

(Goodyear series in education)
1. Teaching–Handbooks, manuals, etc.
2. Handbooks, vade-mecums, etc. I. Gould, Bette Taylor, 1943- joint author.
II. Title.
LB1027.M28 371.3 79-11230
ISBN 0-87620-896-0

Current printing (last digit):
10 9 8 7 6 5 4 3

ISBN: 0-87620-896-0
Y-8960-0

Printed in the United States of America

Art and design: Linda M. Robertson
Production: Project Publishing & Design, Inc.

CONTENTS

INTRODUCTION

This book is a collection of lists. Many of the lists such as Compound Words, Prefixes and Suffixes, and Homonyms are directly connected with the basic skills and content of a school program. Other lists were fun for us to make and have interesting possibilities for classroom use. For example, Flip-Flop Words can be part of a vowel sounds unit and Cockney Rhyming Slang can be used with rhyming words activities. Topics for independent study or research can be selected from lists such as, Words from People's Names, Awards to Animals, and Women.

We have provided worksheets and activities to illustrate the variety of tasks that can be developed from lists. Notes preceding the lists give background information or suggest ways to use the lists.

As a result of using this book, we hope your students will become listmakers. Making lists is a great organizing process and the lists themselves can be effective devices for sharing knowledge. As your students make lists, they'll encounter new sources of information and learn how to use them. There may be instances where they will find points of disagreement between sources which will lead them to check additional references in order to come to a decision on which fact to accept. In the course of list making you may find you've temporarily lost a few listmakers as they become involved in an interesting information source or a list item they wish to pursue further. It's the process that counts here, but the products can be pretty interesting too.

To help get your students started, an A–Z Topics List follows. Any one of the topics on this list can be developed into another list (see the Foods list). The A–Z format is one of the easiest to follow in developing a list. One-item lists such as this can be expanded by adding definitions, descriptions, or other information in either phrase, sentence or paragraph form. As you thumb through the book, you'll see other ways lists can be presented: charts, tables, picture lists and category lists.

As teachers we made and referred to lists all the time. David Wallechinsky and Irving Wallace's *The Book of Lists* motivated us to write *The Teacher's Book of Lists* as a reference for teachers. Some of the lists are standard (Presidents of the U.S., Geometric Formulas); some are extended versions of ones we already had (Compound Words, Consonant Blends); and some were developed on the basis of our own needs and interests (99 Things to Graph and Survey, Hues, Blues and Fugues). We assume that you, as teachers, make or accumulate all sorts of lists. If you have any lists or ideas for lists you'd like to see included in a second edition of *The Teacher's Book of Lists,* write to us c/o Goodyear Publishing Company, 1640 Fifth Street, Santa Monica, California, 90401.

A-Z TOPICS LIST

A actors/actresses, adjectives, airports, announcers (news, sports, etc.)

B bad movies, birds, bones, buildings

C cars, cheeses, chemicals, cities, countries

D dances, dangerous things, dinosaurs, disasters, dogs

E Easter things, egg dishes, energy sources

F fads, foods, football players, furniture pieces

G garden flowers, gargantuan things, gems, German things

H hats, heroes, high places, hobbies, holidays, horses

I ice cream flavors, illnesses, Indian tribes, insects, instruments, inventions

J jams and jellies, jingles, jobs, juices, junk foods

K kids, kings

L lakes, landforms, languages, long and lean things

M Mexican foods, monetary units, monsters, mountains, movies

N names, numbers, nuts

O Olympic events, things you turn on, onomatopoeic names, outfielders

P parks, parties, pets, places, politicians

Q famous quips, T.V. quiz shows

R railroads, things to read, rivers, rocks, roses

S seas, sci-fi words, sculptures, spooky places, sports

T teams, television shows, trees, towers, towns, toys

U undersea dwellers, ungulates, unsafe things, things that go up and down

V Van Gogh's paintings, vegetables, vehicles, verbs

W bodies of water, weather words, worries, writers

X Xmas words, things that are X-rayed

Y things that make you yawn, yellow things

Z zany people, things that zig-zag, things that have a zipper, zoo inhabitants

EAT YOUR WAY THROUGH THE ALPHABET—AN A TO Z LIST OF THINGS TO EAT

Ā apricot

A anchovy, artichoke, asparagus, aspic, avocado

B bacon, bagels, bamboo shoots, bananas, beans, berries, blintzes, bologna, bok choy, bouillon, bread, burritos

hard C cabbage, canapes, cantaloupe, carrots, cauliflower, caviar, clams, cocoa, corn, crab, cranberries, crepes, curry

soft C celery, cereal, ceviche, cilantro, cinnamon

D daikon, dates, dill, doughnuts, duck

Ē ear of corn, Easter eggs, eel

E egg flower soup, eggplant, escargot, escarole

F felafel, figs, filets, fish, fondue, frankfurters, fudge

hard G garbanzo beans, gobo, goose, gooseberries, grapefruit, grapes, gravy

soft G ginger, gingerbread

H hamburgers, hazelnuts, herring, hickory nuts, hominy, honey, horseradish, hot dogs, Hungarian goulash

Ī ice cream, iced tea

Ĭ Indian curry

J jam, jello, jelly, jicama (pronounced *hicama,* could be used under H words)

K kale, ketchup, kreplach, kugel, kumquats

L lasagna, lemonade, lemons, lentils, lichee nuts, lima beans, limes, chopped liver, liverwurst, lobster, lollipops

M macaroni, mango, marshmallows, marzipan, muffins, mushrooms, mustard

N noodles, nuts

Ō oatmeal, okra, oranges

Ŏ octopus, olives, omelette

P papaya, parsley, peanut butter, peanuts, peas, pepper, pickles, pineapples, pita bread, pizza, potatoes, prunes, pudding, pumpkin

Q quail, quince, quinine water

R radishes, raisins, rhubarb, rice, rutabagas

S salami, salt, seaweed, sesame seeds, spaghetti, spinach, squash, squid, steak, stew, succotash

T tea, toast, tofu, tomatoes, tortillas, tuna, turnips, TV dinner

Ŭ upset stomach

V vanilla, vichyssoise, vinegar

W waffles, walnuts, water chestnuts, watercress, watermelon, wild rice, won ton

X e*x*tra helping

Y yam, yeast, yogurt

Z zucchini

THE TEACHER'S BOOK OF LISTS

PART 1

WATCH YOUR LANGUAGE

one
WHAT'S IN A WORD

COMPOUND WORDS

Here is an easy-to-read collection of compounds found in many word lists and beginning readers.

afternoon
airmail
airplane
another
anything
baseball
birthday
blackboard
bluebird
breakfast
busboy
campfire
catfish
chalkboard
classroom
countdown
daytime
dollhouse
doorbell
doorway
downstairs
downtown
driveway
everyone
everywhere
faraway
fireman
fireplace
fisherman
football
footstep
getaway
goldfish
greenhouse
headlight
homework
houseboat
housework
icebox
inside
into
lighthouse
mailbag
mailbox
mailman
maybe
meatballs
moonlight
newspaper
nighttime
nobody
outside
pancake
playground
popcorn
sandbox
sandpaper
schoolhouse
snowball
snowflake
snowman
somebody
someday
someone
something
sometimes
somewhere
spaceman
starfish
sunflower
sunlight
treehouse
upstairs
uptown
wallpaper
workman

. . . . and some more

airport
armchair
ashtray
basketball
bathrobe
bathroom
bedspread
beeswax
bellhop
billboard
blackberry
blueberry
bookcase
bookshelf
breakwater
bridegroom
bridesmaid
butterfly
candlelight
chairperson
checkmate
chestnut
checkout
dashboard
doughnut
driftwood
drugstore
earmuff

earphone
earring
earthquake
eyebrow
fingernail
flashlight
footprint
forehead
freeway
gentleman
grapefruit
grasshopper
Greenland
grownup
hairpin
handcuffs
handkerchief
headache
headquarters
hereinafter
heretofore
highway
homesick
honeymoon
hopscotch
hourglass
housekeeper
hubcap

iceberg
Iceland
kettledrum
keyboard
keyhole
kindergarten
landlady
landlord
landmark
landslide
lifeguard
lipstick
masterpiece
mushroom
necklace
necktie
nickname
nightclub
nightgown
nightmare
notebook
oatmeal
offshore
offspring
outdoors
overcast
passport
password

pawnshop
peanut
pineapple
pocketbook
postcard
racetrack
railroad
rainbow
roadrunner
roommate
sailboat
salesperson
seashell
skateboard
seaway
seaweed
slowpoke
snapdragon
snowstorm
steamboat
stepladder
strawberry
suitcase
sunburn
sunglasses
supermarket
surfboard
swordfish

tattletale
teakettle
teapot
teaspoon
tenderfoot
textbook
thunderbolt
thundercloud
thunderstorm
thunderstruck
timepiece
tiptoe
toothpaste
turnpike
underpants
undershirt
undertaker
upset
wastebasket
waterfall
weekend
wheelchair
whirlpool
wildcat
woodpecker
yourself

Compound Word Activities

1. Classify the words into categories such as people, sports objects, foods, directions, and animals.
2. Illustrate the words.
3. Invent definitions based on the words that make up the compound. (bridesmaid–a woman who washes, cooks, and cleans for a bride)

4. Make new compounds by dividing words and recombining parts to form new words.
   (busboy + doorbell = doorboy, busbell)
5. Write the words that make up the compound.
6. Invent some meaningful three-part compound words and use them in sentences.
   (breakfasttime, airportlane, earphonewire)

SHORT VOWEL/SILENT E PAIRS

Al-ale
at-ate
ban-bane
bar-bare
cam-came
can-cane
cap-cape
car-care
dam-dame
Dan-Dane
fad-fade
fat-fate
fir-fire
flak-flake
gag-gage
gal-gale
gam-game
gap-gape
hat-hate
Jan-Jane
lam-lame
mad-made
man-mane
mar-mare

mat-mate
nap-nape
pal-pale
pan-pane
par-pare
past-paste
pat-pate
plan-plane
rag-rage
rat-rate
sag-sage
Sam-same
sat-sate
slat-slate
spat-spate
stag-stage
tam-tame
tap-tape
van-vane
wag-wage
wan-wane
met-mete
pet-Pete

con-cone
cop-cope
cot-cote
dot-dote
glob-globe
hop-hope
lop-lope
mop-mope
not-note
pop-pope
rod-rode
rot-rote
ton-tone
tot-tote
bid-bide
bit-bite
dim-dime
din-dine
fin-fine
grim-grime
grip-gripe
jib-jibe

kit-kite
mit-mite
pin-pine
pip-pipe
quit-quite
rid-ride
rip-ripe
shin-shine
sin-sine
sir-sire
sit-site
slid-slide
slim-slime
spit-spite
strip-stripe
Tim-time
tin-tine
trip-tripe
twin-twine
win-wine
cut-cute
hug-huge
jut-jute
us-use

PREFIXES AND SUFFIXES

Definitions for these common prefixes and suffixes have been simplified. Only the most frequently used meanings of the prefixes and suffixes have been selected for the list. The words given as examples generally contain a root word that children can easily identify.

Prefixes

AD-, AC-

1. to, toward: *ad*verb, *ad*equate, *ac*credit, *ac*custom
2. near: *ad*renal

ANTE-

1. before, prior: *ante*date
2. in front of: *ante*chamber, *ante*room

ANTI-

1. against, opposite of, in opposition to: *anti*slavery, *anti*freeze, *anti*climax, *anti*aircraft

BI-

1. two: *bi*cycle, *bi*annual
2. twice during every or once in every two: *bi*weekly, *bi*monthly

CIRCUM-

1. around: *circum*navigate, *circum*lunar

CO-, COM-, CON-

1. with, together: *co*exist, *com*patriot, *con*form

CONTRA-, COUNTER-

1. against, opposite: *contra*diction, *counter*balance, *counter*clockwise

DE-

1. opposite of: *de*code
2. remove from: *de*horn, *de*throne
3. reduce or lower: *de*flate, *de*grade

DEC-, DECA-, DEKA-

1. ten: *dec*ade, *deca*liter

DIS-

1. not, opposite of, reverse: *dis*belief, *dis*orderly, *dis*approve

2. apart, away from: *dis*lodge

EN-
1. put on or into: *en*throne, *en*danger, *en*act
2. cover or surround: *en*close, *en*wrap, *en*fold, *en*circle, *en*compass, *en*gulf
3. make: *en*able, *en*large

EX-
1. former, before: *ex*president
2. from, out of, beyond: *ex*change, *ex*hale, *ex*port

EXTRA-, EXTRO-
1. beyond, outside the scope or region of, besides: *extra*sensory, *extra*ordinary, *extro*vert

HYPER-
1. more than usual, in excess: *hyper*active, *hyper*critical, *hyper*sensitive

HYPO-
1. under, beneath: *hypo*dermic

IN-, IM-
1. not, without: *in*active, *im*possible

IN-, INTRA-
1. in, into, within: *in*born, *intra*spinal

INTER-
1. jointly, together: *inter*lace, *inter*twine
2. between or among: *inter*island, *inter*continental

MID-
1. middle: *mid*way, *mid*town, *mid*term, *mid*summer, *mid*brain, *mid*day

MIS-
1. wrong, wrongly: *mis*quote, *mis*advise, *mis*copy, *mis*inform, *mis*judge, *mis*read, *mis*pronounce
2. bad, badly: *mis*fortune, *mis*treat, *mis*adventure, *mis*shapen, *mis*conduct

MONO-

1. one, single: *mono*rail, *mono*tone

NON-

1. not: *non*fiction, *non*-American, *non*conformity, *non*breakable

OUT-

1. greater, better: *out*distance, *out*dance, *out*run, *out*fight, *out*do, *out*live
2. outer place: *out*doors, *out*side, *out*field, *out*post

OVER-

1. beyond, too much: *over*eat, *over*act, *over*heat, *over*ripe, *over*sleep

POST-

1. after, later: *post*war
2. positioned behind: *post*dental

PRE-

1. before or at an earlier time: *pre*school, *pre*historic, *pre*mature
2. in front of: *pre*fix

PRO-

1. for, in favor of: *pro*-American, *pro*-labor

RE-

1. again: *re*do, *re*finish
2. back: *re*turn, *re*bound, *re*call

RETRO-

1. backward: *retro*gress, *retro*active, *retro*rocket

SUB-

1. under: *sub*soil, *sub*way
2. not up to, inadequate, less than: *sub*standard, *sub*normal
3. part of a whole: *sub*station, *sub*culture, *sub*district, *sub*committee

TRANS-
1. move from one place to another: *trans*plant
2. across: *trans*continental, *trans*atlantic, *trans*oceanic
3. change: *trans*form, *trans*figuration

TRI-
1. three: *tri*colored, *tri*lingual, *tri*angle, *tri*motor
2. once in every three: *tri*monthly
3. three times during every: *tri*weekly, *tri*annual

UN-
1. not, opposite of: *un*clean, *un*clear
2. reverse or opposite of an action: *un*button, *un*pack
3. lack of: *un*easy, *un*rest

Suffixes

-ABLE, -BLE, -IBLE
1. able to, capable of, possible to: erase*able*, reproduc*ible*
2. tending or likely to: peace*able,* perish*able*

-AL
1. belonging to, having the characteristics of: music*al*, norm*al*, industri*al*, trib*al*
2. process of action: refus*al*, arriv*al*

-ANCE, -ANCY, -ENCE, -ENCY
1. quality, act, or condition: resist*ance*, assist*ance*, depend*ence,* emerg*ency*

-ANT, -ENT
1. be in or perform a certain act: serv*ant*, deodor*ant*, solv*ent*

-ATE
1. result or act of, provide with: refriger*ate*, hyphen*ate*

-DOM
1. area ruled by: king*dom*
2. condition or state of being: free*dom*, martyr*dom*

-ESS
1. female: godd*ess*, host*ess* lion*ess*

-EST
1. superlative of adjectives: bigg*est*, slow*est*, small*est*, healthi*est*

-FUL
1. full of: joy*ful*, beauti*ful*
2. character of: shame*ful*, grace*ful*, man*ful*
3. quantity that would fill: cup*ful*

-FY
1. to form into or become: beauti*fy*, classi*fy*, lique*fy*, nulli*fy*, sissi*fy*, solidi*fy*

-HOOD
1. state of being: child*hood*, man*hood*
2. membership in a group: brother*hood*, priest*hood*

-IC
1. pertaining to, of, part of: angel*ic*, alcohol*ic*, volcan*ic*

-ICS
1. art, science, study of: ceram*ics*, systemat*ics*, tact*ics*
2. act or practice of: athlet*ics*, gymnast*ics*

-ISH
1. nationality: Turk*ish*, Scott*ish*
2. likeness to: mann*ish*, clown*ish*, child*ish*
3. somewhat: brown*ish*, warm*ish*, tall*ish*

-IVE
1. having the quality of: mass*ive*
2. tending to: disrupt*ive*, instruct*ive*

-LESS
1. lack of, without: penni*less*, head*less*, shoe*less*, shirt*less*, meat*less*

-LET
1. smallness in size or importance: play*let*, leaf*let*
2. worn on the body: ank*let*

-LIKE
1. similar to: child*like*, life*like*

-LY
1. in a certain manner: sad*ly*, quick*ly*, efficient*ly*
2. like, having a resemblance to: man*ly*, queen*ly*
3. occurring every: year*ly*, month*ly*
4. in a certain place: third*ly*

-MENT
1. result of, thing produced by: engage*ment*, entangle*ment*
2. process or act of: develop*ment*, detach*ment*
3. state, quality, or condition of: amaze*ment*, enjoy*ment*

-NESS
1. manner or state of being: dark*ness*, unhappi*ness*

-OR
1. person or thing that performs: audit*or*, creat*or*, escalat*or*, govern*or*, investigat*or*
2. state, manner, or act: err*or*, pall*or*

-SHIP
1. state of: kin*ship*, friend*ship*
2. office, rank, level: intern*ship*, lord*ship*
3. art or skill: author*ship*, horseman*ship*, marksman*ship*

-TION, -SION
1. action or process of: pronuncia*tion*, rejec*tion*
2. condition: comple*tion*, starva*tion*, confu*sion*
3. result of: discus*sion*, transla*tion*

-TY, -ITY
1. state, quality, or amount: fals*ity*, humid*ity*, safe*ty*, mediocr*ity*, obes*ity*, inferior*ity*
2. 10 times: six*ty*

-WARD, -WARDS
1. toward, in the direction of: back*wards*, north*ward*

-WISE
1. way, direction, or manner: counterclock*wise*, length*wise*
2. in respect to: time*wise*, money*wise*

-Y, -EY
1. characterized by, resembling, having: rain*y*, storm*y*, slim*y*, thirst*y*
2. quality or state of: jealous*y*, victor*y*
3. act, place, or business: baker*y*
4. little or small: bunn*y*, pant*y*

WORDS FROM PEOPLE'S NAMES

Sylvester Graham (1794–1851) advocated a vegetarian diet and other natural foods. His followers ate unleavened biscuits made of whole grain flour that were called graham crackers. Many other words we use have come from people's names. Here are 70 more.

ampere
babbitt
begonia
bloomers
boycott
boysenberry
braille
bunsen burner
camellia
cardigan
cereal
chauvinist
daguerrotype
dahlia
diesel engine
doily
dunce
fahrenheit
ferris wheel
forsythia
fuchsia
gaillardia
galvanize
gardenia
gerrymandering
guillotine
hooligan
kaiser
loganberry
lothario
lynch
macadam
machiavellian
mackintosh
magnolia
malthusian
marcel
marconigram
masochistic
maverick
melba toast
mercerize
nicotine
ohm
pasteurize
poinsettia
pollyanna
pompadour
praline
pullman
quisling
raglan
sadist
sandwich
saxophone
sequoia
shrapnel
silhouette
spoonerism
St. Bernard dog
teddy bear
timothy
titian
Tommy Atkins
tommy-gun
victorian
volt
watt
wisteria
zeppelin

LATIN AND GREEK STEMS

Latin Stems

ACT (do, drive)
actor, deactivate, reaction

AQUA (water)
aquarium, aquanaut, aqueduct

AUDI (hear)
audio, audition, audience

CENT (hundred)
centipede, cent, century

CREAT (make)
creation, creative, recreation

DIC, DICT (say, speak, declare)
diction, dictator, indictment, prediction

DUC, DUCT (lead, draw, bring, take)
produce, productive, aqueduct, deduct

EQU (same, even)
equity, equation, equator, unequal, equilateral

FER (carry, bring)
transfer, ferry

FLEX (bend)
flexible, reflection

FRACT (break)
fragile, fragment, fraction, fracture

FUSE (pour)
transfusion, refuse, confused

GRESS (step, go)
progress, aggressive, digress

JECT (throw)
project, inject, subject, eject

LIBER (free)
liberation, liberal, liberty

LOC (place)
location, local, locate

MAL (bad)
malice, malign, malediction

MANU (hand)
manipulate, manuscript, manual, manufacture

MARE (sea)
marine, submarine, maritime aquamarine

MEM (keep in mind)
memory, memorize, remember

MIT (go, send)
remit, transmitter, admit, emit

MOB, MOT, MOV (move, movable)
mobile, motor, promoted, automobile

OCTO (eight)
octave, octet, octagon, octopus, octogenarian

PED (foot)
pedal, pedestal

PEL (push, drive)
propel, expel, repelled

PEND (hang)
append, pendant, dependent, suspend

PLI (fold)
pliable, duplicate, complicate

PORT (carry)
portable, export, report, import

SCRIB, SCRIPT (write)
prescription, postscript, describe

UNI (one, single)
uniform, reunite, unicycle, unity

VAC (empty)
vacate, vacuum, evacuate

VIS (see)
vision, vista, revise, invisible

Greek Stems

astro (star): astrology, astronomy, astrologer

auto (self): autograph, autobiography, automobile

bio (life, living things): biography, biology, biopsy

geo (earth, land): geography, geometry, geology

gram (something written down, drawn, or recorded): telegram, electrocardiogram

graph (something that writes, written): autograph, photograph, telegraph

gyro, gyr (circle, spiral): gyroscope, gyrate

hemi (half): hemisphere

hydro (water): hydrofoil, hydrogen, hydrophone

meter (measure): speedometer, odometer

micro (small): microscope, microphone, microfilm

mono (single, one): monotone, monograph, monogram

ology, logy (study of, science of): biology, geology, psychology

phone (sound, voice): microphone, telephone, phonograph

photo (light): photograph, phototype

poly (many, much): polyhedron

scope (instrument for seeing or observing): telescope, microscope

sphere (ball, globe): atmosphere, hydrosphere

tele (far away, distant): teletype, television, telegram

therm, thermo (heat): thermometer, thermostat

zoo (animal): zoo, zoology, zoography

Name

ANTONYM ALBUM

Look at the pictures on this album page. Label each picture with a pair of antonyms.

CONSONANT BLENDS/DIGRAPHS

These words have been arranged so that short-vowel words are listed first.

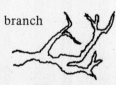

BL

blink
blast
bless
blunt
blotter
bleed
blow
blame
blind

block

blanket

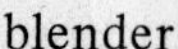

blender

BR

brat
breath
brig
brought
brunt
brave
breed
bright
broken
brood
brown

bread

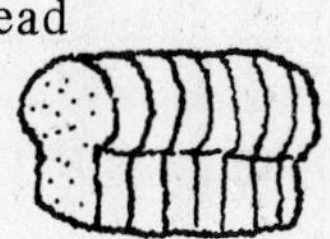

branch

bridge

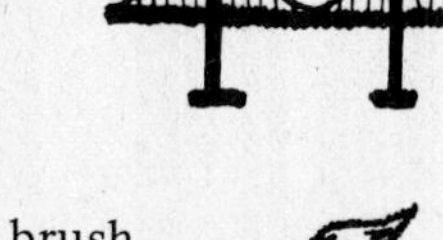

brush

broom

CL

clap
clement
clip
clod
closet
club
clay
clean
climb
cloak
clue
clout

claw

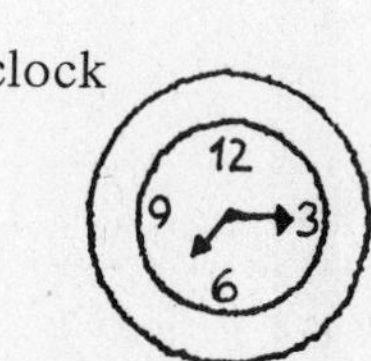

clock

cloud

CR

crack
crest
crib
crop
crumb
crazy
creed
crime
croak
crew
crawl
crowd

crab

cradle

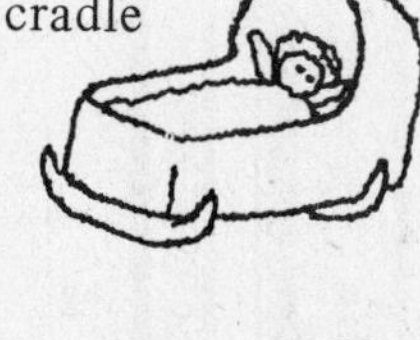

crayon

cross

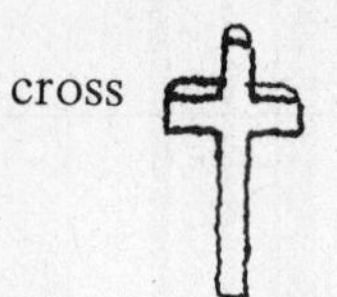

cry

DR

drab
drift
dread
drawl
droop
drake
dream
drive
drone
drew
drought

drip
dress
dropper
drum

FL

flat
flesh
fling
flop
flutter
flake
flea
flier
float
fluke
flour

flag
fly
flame
flower

FR

fragment
fresh
friend
frill
frost
frustrate
freight
freeze
fry
frozen
frugal

frog
frown
fruit

GL

glad
glen
glisten
glob
glutton
glade
glee
glide
glow
glue
gloom

gloves

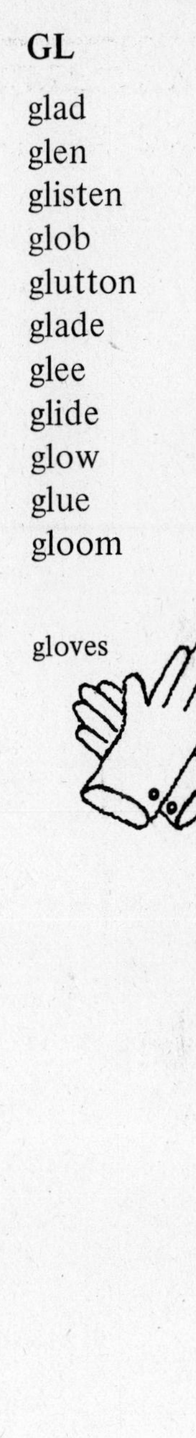

GR

gratis
grid
grovel
grip
grate
grease
grind
groan
group
groom
growl

grass

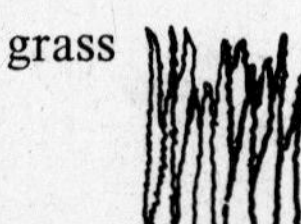

grapes

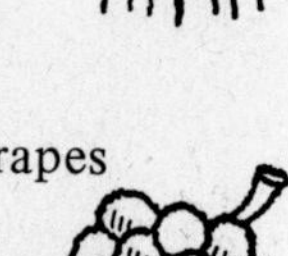

PL

plank
plastic
pledge
plod
pluck
plunder
play
plead
please
ply
Pluto
ploy

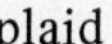

plaid

plate

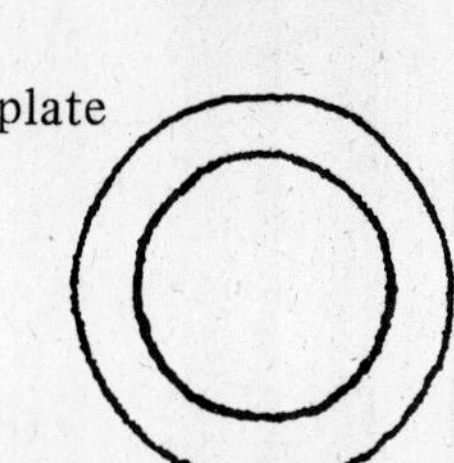

plow

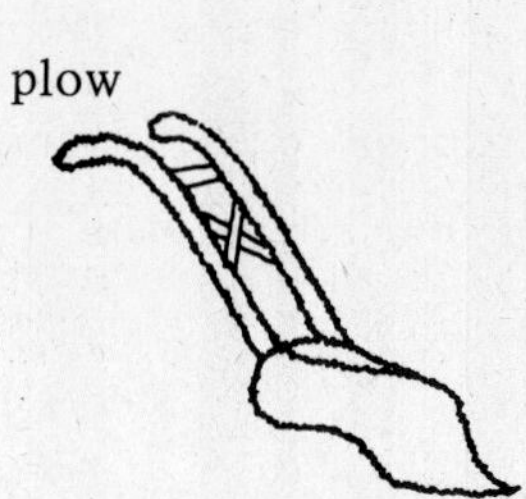

PR

practice
press
prison
principal
prod
pray
preen
pride
probe
prune
prowl
proof

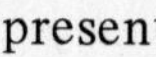

present

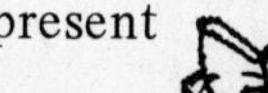

SC, SK

scamp
scat
scare
scope
scold
scowl
skim
skin
skip
skeleton
skeptical

scarf

ski

skates

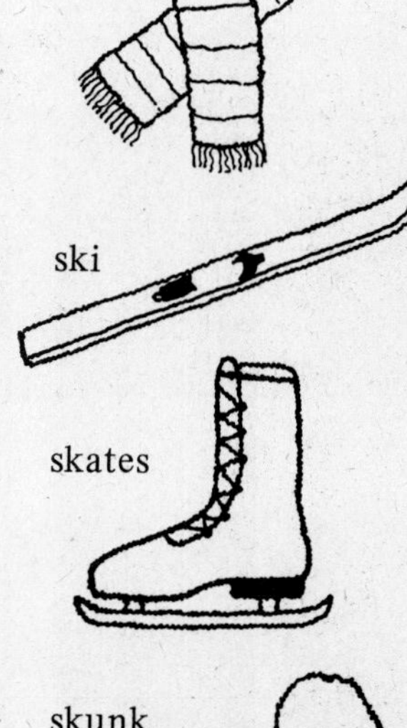

skunk

skull

SL

slam
slept
slit
slot
slumber
slate
sleep
slice
slope
sloop

SM

smash
smack
smell
Smith
small
smog
smug
smear
smooth

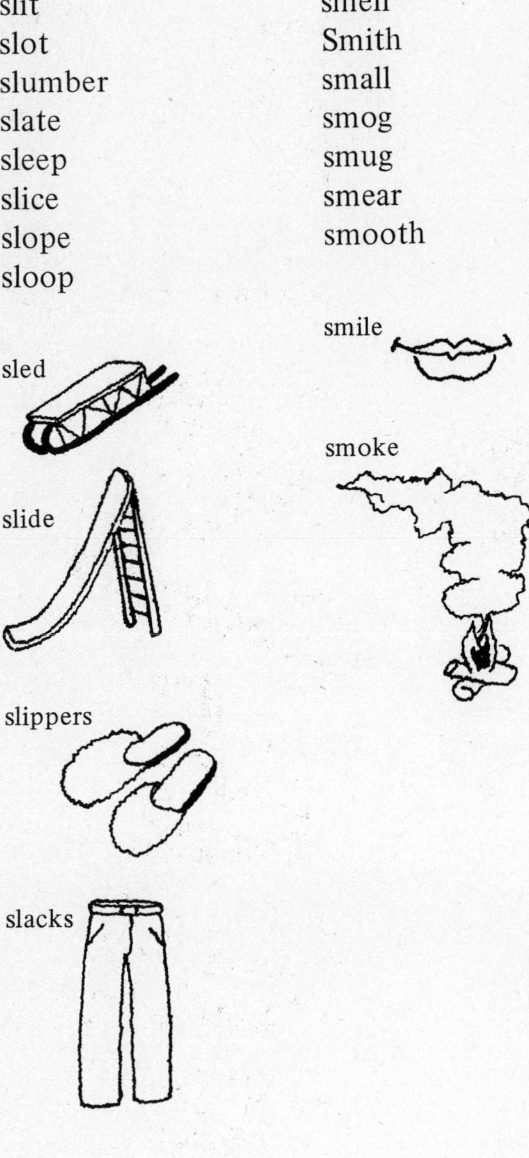

SN

snag
snip
snuff
snuggle
sneak
snide
snoop
snout
snare

SP

spank
spatter
sped
spill
Sputnik
spunk
space
speak
spy
spore
spew
spoil

ST

staff
stab
standard
steps
stick
stock
stumble
stare
steel
style
stole
student
stoop

star

stop sign

steak

stool

stove

SW

swam
swell
swift
swim
sway
sweet
swipe
swollen
swoon
swoop

sweater

swan

swing

TR

traffic
trap
trend
tread
trinket
trip
trod
tropical
trump
trust
trail
treat
tribe
troll
true
trouble
trout

track

truck

tree

tricycle

train

TW

twist
twinkle
twitch
twill
twain
tweed
tweak
tweet
twice
twine

twenty

twelve

tweezers

twig

twins

QU

quarrel
question
quickly
quit
quake
quite
quote

queen

quail

SPL

splash
splendid
split
splint
splotch
spleen
splice
splurge

splinter

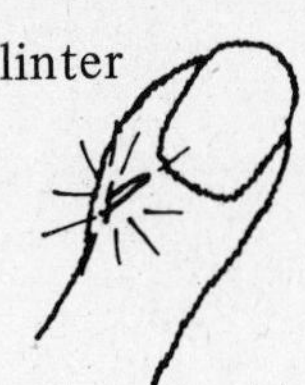

SCR

scrap
scramble
scrimmage
script
scrub
scrape
screen
scream
scribe

scroll

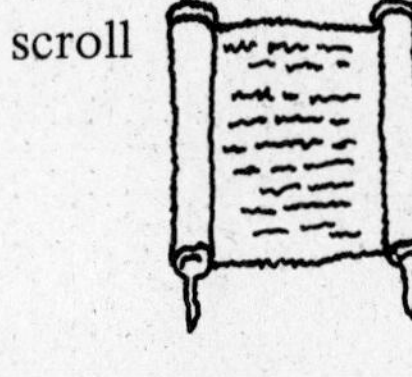

screw

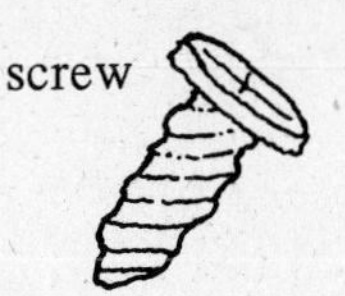

SPR

spread
sprig
sprinkle
sprocket
sprung
sprain
spray
spree
spritely
spry

spring

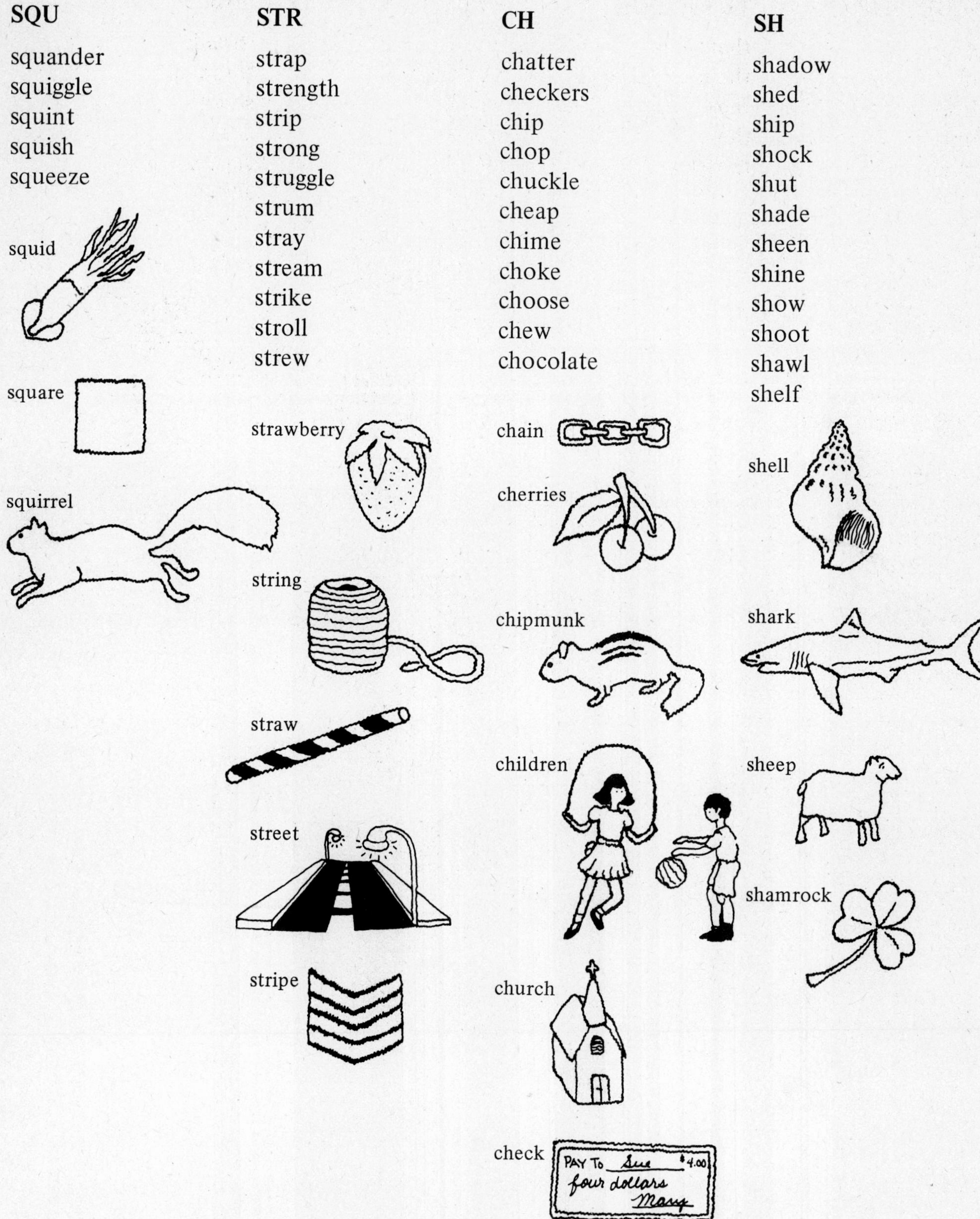
SQU
squander
squiggle
squint
squish
squeeze
squid
square
squirrel
STR
strap
strength
strip
strong
struggle
strum
stray
stream
strike
stroll
strew
strawberry
string
straw
street
stripe
CH
chatter
checkers
chip
chop
chuckle
cheap
chime
choke
choose
chew
chocolate
chain
cherries
chipmunk
children
church
check
PAY To Sue $4.00
four dollars
Mary
SH
shadow
shed
ship
shock
shut
shade
sheen
shine
show
shoot
shawl
shelf
shell
shark
sheep
shamrock

TH (unvoiced)	**TH (voiced)**	**WH**	**SHR**
thatch	that	when	shrank
thin	them	whether	shrapnel
think	then	which	shred
thunder	there	where	shrill
thought	they	whine	shrink
thief		white	shrub

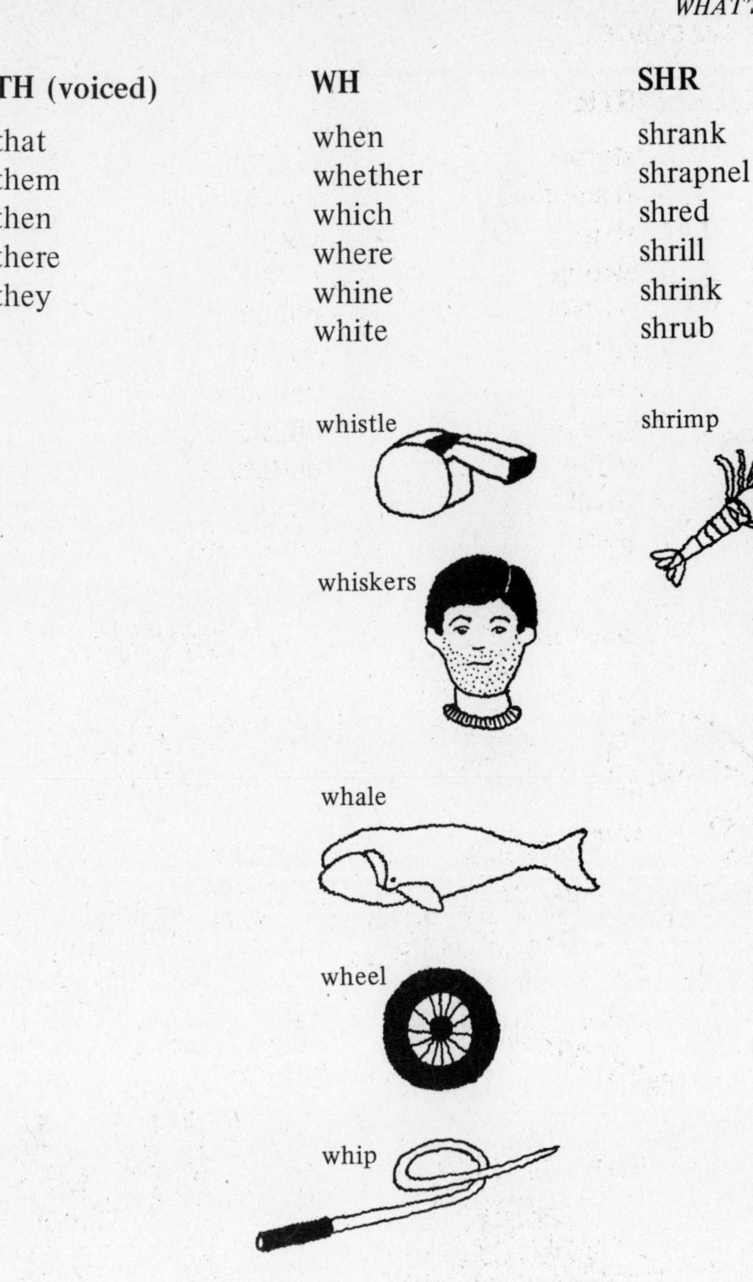

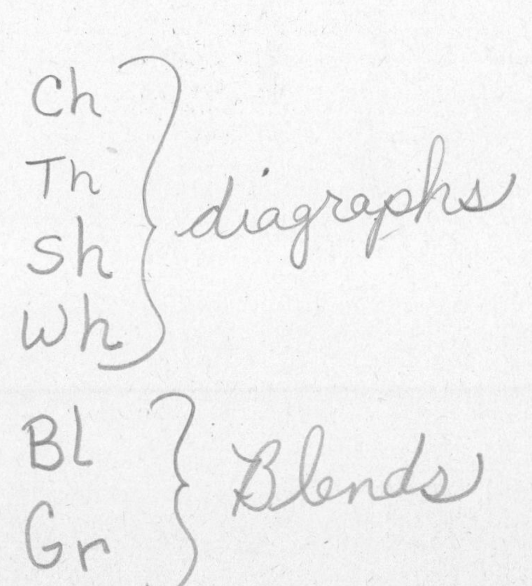

WORD ENDINGS

-FT

craft
cleft
drift
sift
soft
tuft

raft

-MP

champ
cramp
ramp
hemp
limp
romp
dump
hump

lamp

chimp

shrimp

-ND

band
land
sand
wind
kind
pound
round

wand

pond

-NG

bang
sting
string
long
wrong
hung
lung

ring

king

wing

-NK

tank
spank
link
shrink
honk
chunk
junk

sink

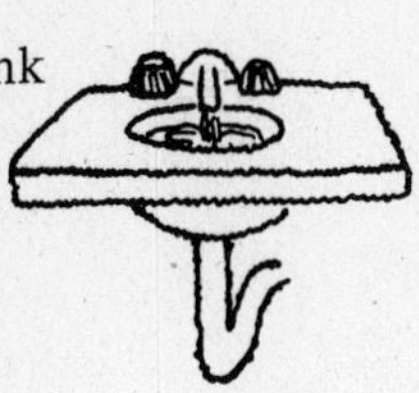

skunk

trunk

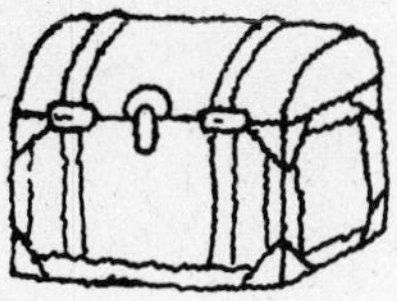

-NT

slant
bent
hint
tint
front
hunt
runt

tent

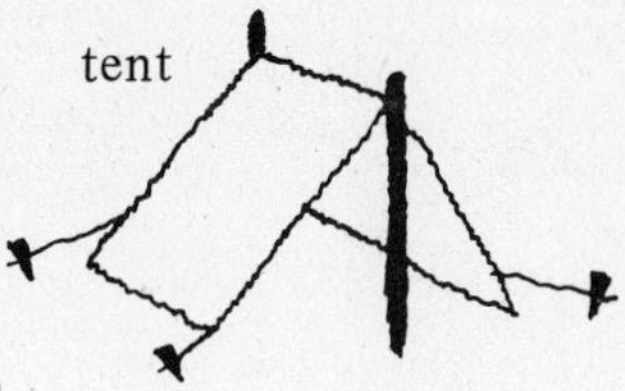

plant

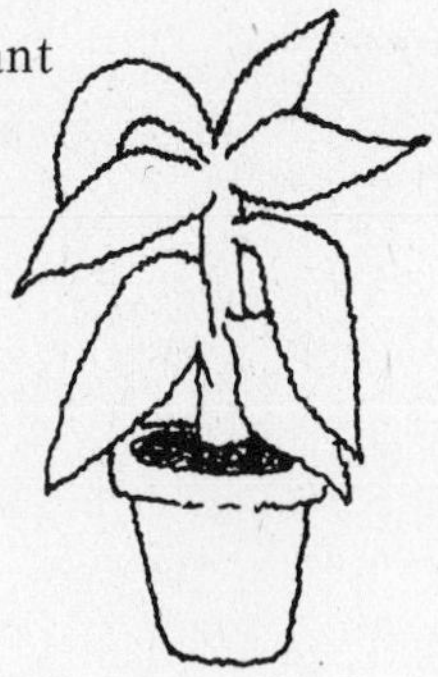

paint

present

-SK

flask
task
risk
whisk
husk
tusk
kiosk

mask

desk

-SP

asp
rasp
clasp
grasp
crisp

-ST

last
best
mist
cost
rust
waist
least
coast
roost

fist

wrist

-CH

crunch
teach
coach
porch
couch
ouch
staunch

church

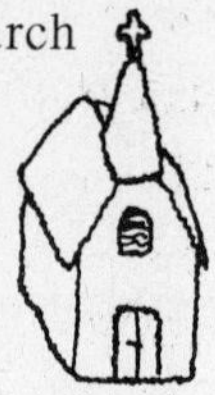

peach

-SH

crash
flesh
mesh
wish
gosh
crush
rush
wash

fish

dish

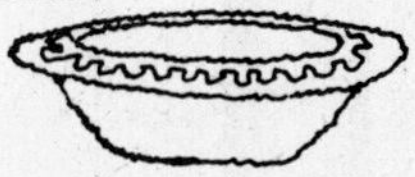

-TH

bath
path
breath
tenth
month
faith
tooth
truth
uncouth

mouth

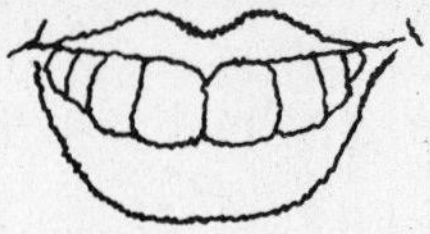

teeth

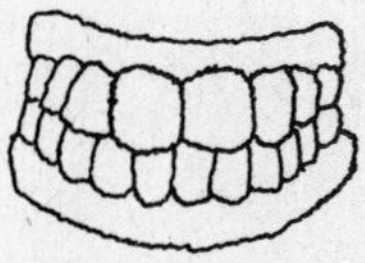

VOWEL DIGRAPH AND DIPHTHONG WORDS

Digraphs

ai as in sail	ay as in day	ea as in team	ea as in head	ea as in break
afraid	clay	cream	bread	steak
aim	crayon	deal	feather	
chain	gray	easy	heather	
fail	lay	flea	lead	
jail	may	gleam	measure	
maize	play	grease	read	
paid	prayer	leak	tread	
paint	slay	mean	treasure	
praise	stay	peak	weather	
proclaim	sway	plead		
rain	tray	preach		
snail		repeal		
stain		seam		
straight		squeal		
train		teach		

ee as in week	ei as in eight	ey as in key	ie as in piece	oa as in boat
flee	freight	donkey	belief	coat
free	neigh	honey	chief	float
glee	neighbor	monkey	lien	load
green	rein	trolley	relief	moat
heed	skein	volley		poach
need	sleigh			road
queen	vein			roam
seed				soak
sheen				toad
sheet				
sneeze				
steed				
sweet				
three				
tree				

oo as in foot	**oo as in moon**	**ow as in crow**	**ue as in blue**
book	balloon	blow	due
cook	bassoon	flow	glue
crook	croon	low	gruesome
good	fool	mow	sue
hood	hoot	row	true
look	room	slow	
shook	school	throw	
stood	shoot	tow	
took	spoon		
wood	stool		
	swoon		
	too		
	tool		
	toot		
	zoo		

Digraphs followed by r

air as in pair	**ear as in year**	**ear as in earth**	**ear as in bear**	**eer as in deer**
eclair	appear	Earl	pear	beer
fair	beard	early	tear	cheer
flair	clear	earn	swear	leer
hair	dear	heard	wear	peer
lair	dreary	hearse		queer
stair	ear	learn		seer
	fear	pearl		sheer
	gear	search		steer
	hear			
	near			
	rear			
	spear			
	tear			

ier as in pier

fierce
pierce
tier

oar as in oar

boar
roar
soar

our as in four

pour

Diphthongs

au as in taught

caught
flaunt
haul
haunt
maul
pauper
sausage
taut

aw as in saw

crawl
draw
drawl
fawn
gawk
hawk
law
lawn
raw
shawl
straw
tawny
yawn

ew as in grew

blew
crew
dew
drew
flew
new
slew
stew
threw

oi as in oil

avoid
coil
coin
foil
hoist
join
loin
loiter
noise
point
poison
soil
spoil
toil
voice

ou as in out

blouse
cloud
couch
foul
house
loud
mouth
mouse
ouch
pouch
pound
round
shout
south
trout

ow as in cow

down
drown
flower
fowl
frown
gown
how
plow
renown
shower
town
trowel

oy as in boy

coy
destroy
employ
enjoy
joy
ploy
Roy
toy
voyage

SILENTS, PLEASE—COMMON SILENT LETTERS

silent gh	gn, silent g	kn, silent k	wr, silent w	mb, silent b
bought	gnarl	knack	wrap	bomb
caught	gnash	knapsack	wreath	climb
dough	gnat	knave	wreck	comb
eight	gnaw	knead	wren	crumb
flight	gneiss	knee	wrench	jamb
high	gnome	knew	wrestle	lamb
right	gnu	knife	wring	limb
sleigh	align	knight	wrinkle	numb
sigh	arraign	knit	wrist	thumb
taught	feign	knob	write	tomb
thought	reign	knock	wrong	
	sign	knot	wrote	
		know		
		knowledge		
		knuckle		

TONGUE TWISTERS FROM A TO Z

In 1819, *Peter Piper's Practical Principles of Plain and Perfect Pronunciation* was published in England by J. Harris and Son. The book contained a tongue twister for each letter of the alphabet. Of these, "Peter Piper" still remains. Here are our new first lines for tongue twisters for each letter of the alphabet. In order to complete them, follow this pattern for "Peter Piper."

The first line is a statement.	Peter Piper picked a peck of pickled peppers.
The second line asks if the statement is true.	Did Peter Piper pick a peck of pickled peppers?
The third and fourth lines ask an "if" and "where" question.	If Peter Piper picked a peck of pickled peppers, where's the peck of pickled peppers Peter Piper picked?

Angela Abigail Applewhite ate anchovies and artichokes.

Bertha Bartholomew blew blue bubbles.

Clifford Cleaver clumsily closed the closet clasp.

Dwayne Dwiddle drew a drawing of dreaded Dracula.

Elmer Elwood eluded eleven elderly elephants.

Floyd Flingle flipped flat flapjacks.

Greta Gruber grabbed a group of green grapes.

Hattie Henderson hated happy hippos.

Ida Ivy identified the ivory iris.

Julie Jackson juggled the juicy, jiggly jello.

Karl Kessler kept the ketchup in the kitchen.

Lela Ladder lugged a lot of little lemons.

Milton Mallard mailed a mangled mango.

Newton Norton never needed new noodles.

Oscar Oliver ought to auction odd objects.

Patsy Planter plucked plump, purple, plastic plums.

Quincy Quist quite quickly quelled the quarreling quartet.

Randy Rathbone wrapped a rather rare red rabbit.

Shelly Sherman shivered in a sheer, short shirt.

Trina Tweety tripped two twittering twins under a twiggy tree.

Uri Udall usually used his unicycle.

Vicky Vine viewed a very valuable vase.

Walter Worple warily warned the weary warrior.

Xerxes Xenon expected to xerox extra x-rays.

Yolanda Yarger yodeled yonder yesterday.

Ziggy Zine zig-zagged through the zoo zone.

Tongue-Twisting Activities

1. Make up twisters about people you know.
2. Make up twisters about products you use.
3. Make up a second line for a twister that does *not* follow the Peter Piper pattern.

   Hattie Henderson hated happy hippos.
   She hoped the hippos had a horrible holiday.
4. Illustrate the twisters.
5. Extend the twisters by adding adjectives and adverbs to them.

   Angela Abigail Applewhite *artfully* ate *angular* anchovies and *awesome* artichokes.
6. Complete each tongue twister in the form of "Peter Piper."

WORD TWINS, TRIPLETS, AND QUADRUPLETS

Twins

aches and pains
Aunt and Uncle

back and forth
black and blue
black and white
blood and guts
bread and butter
bright and shiny
bright-eyed and bushy-tailed

cake and ice cream
cat and mouse
cease and desist
chips and dip
cloak and dagger
coat and tie
cold and clammy
cops and robbers
cowboys and Indians
cup and saucer
cut and dried
cut and paste

dogs and cats
do's and don'ts

ebb and flow

fish and chips
foot-loose and fancy-free

hearts and flowers
hide and seek
high and dry
high and mighty
hill and dale
hither and yon
huff and puff
hugs and kisses

in and out

jump and shout

knife and fork

lathe and plaster
life and death
light and fluffy
long and short
lost and found
loud and clear

Mom and Dad
Mother and Father

nickel and dime
night and day
now or never
nuts and bolts

old and gray
on and off
open and closed
open and shut

paper and pencil
peace and quiet
pins and needles
potatoes and gravy
p's and q's

read and write
rest and relaxation
rise and fall
rise and shine
rough and ready

safe and sound
salt and pepper
shoes and socks
short but sweet
show and tell
slip and slide
sister and brother
soap and water
sound and fury
soup to nuts
spic and span
sticks and stones
stop and go
strange but true
strong and silent
sugar and spice

table and chairs
tortoise and the hare
toss and turn

up and down

vinegar and oil

wash and dry
whether or not
wild and wooly

Triplets

animal, vegetable or mineral

bacon, lettuce and tomato
bell, book and candle

coffee, tea or milk

hop, skip and a jump

men, women and children

reading, writing and arithmetic
red, white and blue

snap, crackle and pop

tall, dark and handsome

up, up and away

Quadruplets

ear, eyes, nose and throat
eeny, meeny, miney, moe

rain, hail, sleet or snow
rich man, poor man,
beggarman, thief

Activities With Word Twins, Triplets, and Quadruplets

1. List word pairs that can be reversed, such as night and day, cats and dogs, and sister and brother.
2. Group word pairs into categories such as foods, people, directions, and actions.
3. Use word pairs in sentences.
4. List word pairs that are opposites, such as long and short or rise and fall.
5. Find word pairs that repeat the same word, such as over and over, coast to coast, and higher and higher.
6. Find people that are often thought of in twosomes or threesomes, such as Laurel and Hardy, Sonny and Cher, and Larry, Moe, and Curly Joe.

Name

WORD TWINS CROSSWORD

Work the crossword puzzle by filling in the word that completes each twin or triplet.

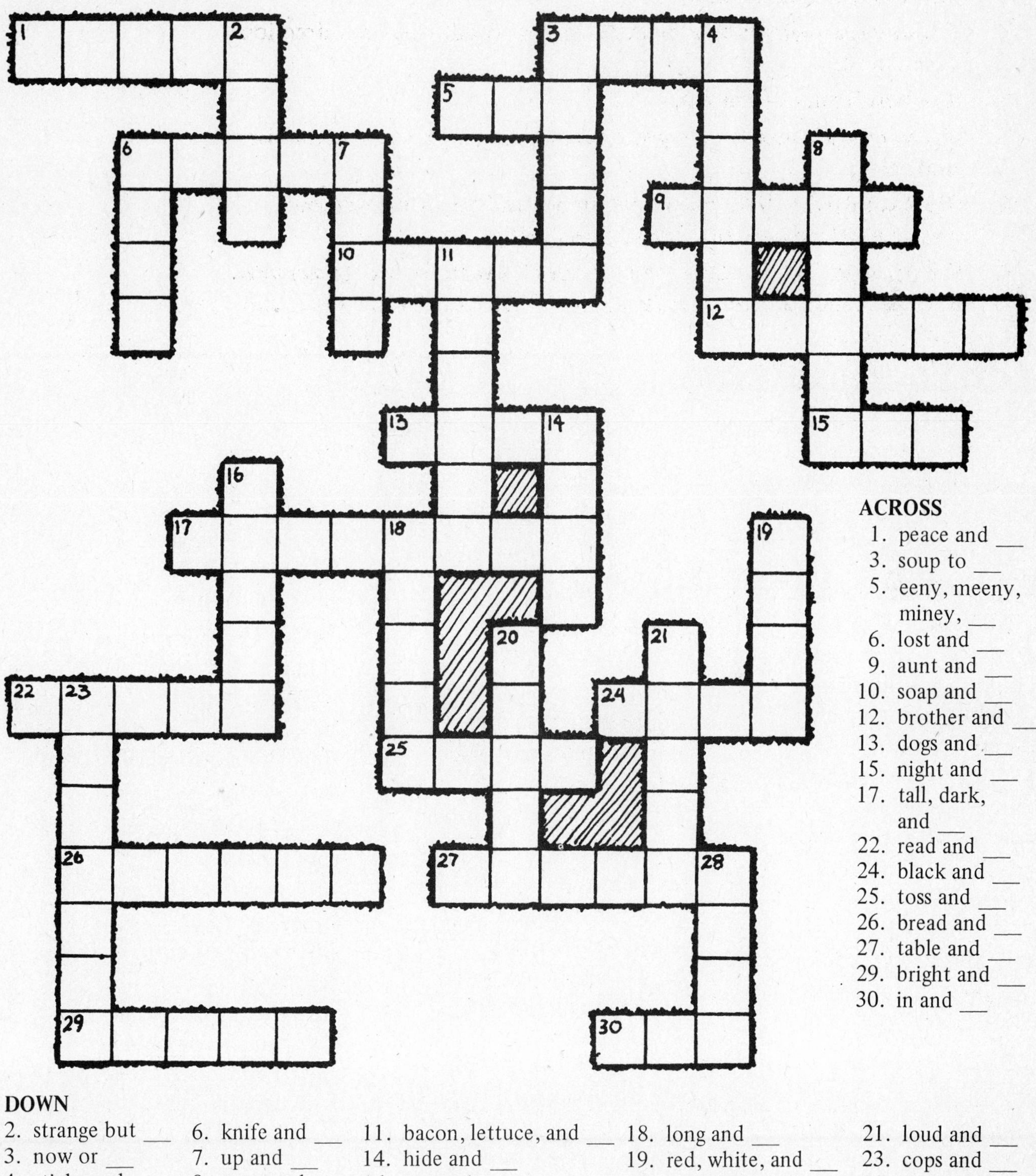

ACROSS

1. peace and ___
3. soup to ___
5. eeny, meeny, miney, ___
6. lost and ___
9. aunt and ___
10. soap and ___
12. brother and ___
13. dogs and ___
15. night and ___
17. tall, dark, and ___
22. read and ___
24. black and ___
25. toss and ___
26. bread and ___
27. table and ___
29. bright and ___
30. in and ___

DOWN

2. strange but ___
3. now or ___
4. sticks and ___
6. knife and ___
7. up and ___
8. open and ___
11. bacon, lettuce, and ___
14. hide and ___
16. cut and ___
18. long and ___
19. red, white, and ___
20. back and ___
21. loud and ___
23. cops and ___
28. open and ___

two

WHAT'S NOT IN A WORD

ABBR.—ABBREVIATIONS

These often-used abbreviations are listed with their most common meanings. Many abbreviations have more than one meaning, such as *cont.* for continued, contents, and continent.

acct.—account
a.m.—before noon
anon.—anonymous
approx.—approximate
appt.—appointment
apt.—apartment
arr.—arrival
assn., assoc.—association
asst.—assistant
attn.—attention
atty.—attorney
Ave.—Avenue
avg.—average

beg.—beginning
bet.—between
bldg.—building
Blvd.—Boulevard

cc—carbon copy
chs.—chapters
clsd.—closed
Co.—Company
Corp.—Corporation
ctr.—center

dbl.—double
dent.—dentist
dep.—departure
dept.—department
Dr.—Doctor

E.—East
ea.—each
e.g.—for example
elem.—elementary
encl.—enclosure
ency.—encyclopedia
env.—envelope
est.—established
etc.—and so forth (etcetera)

Frwy.—Freeway

govt.—government

hosp.—hospital
Hwy.—Highway

ibid.—in the same place (ibidem)
id.—the same (idem)
illus.—illustration, illustrated
init.—initial

misc.—miscellaneous
mo.—month
mfg.—manufacturing
mgr.—manager
Mr.—form of address for a man
Mrs.—form of address for a married woman
Ms.—form of address for a woman

Mt., mts.–Mount, mountains
no.–number
N., No.–North
nos.–numbers
obs.–obsolete
p.–page
pd.–paid
perm.–permanent
pkg.–package
Pkwy.–Parkway
p.m.–after noon
pp.–pages
pr.–pair
recd.–received
Rd.–Road
rt.–right
Rte.–Route
S., So.–South
sta.–station
stmt.–statement
tel. no.–telephone number
v., vs.–versus
vocab.–vocabulary
W.–West
wk., wks.–week, weeks
w/–with
w/o–without
yrs.–yours
a.k.a.–also known as
a.s.a.p.–as soon as possible
b.l.t.–bacon, lettuce, tomato (sandwich)
c/o–care of
c.o.d.–cash on delivery
i.d.–identification
I.O.U.–I owe you
I.Q.–intelligence quotient
k.o.–knock out
m.p.g.–miles per gallon
m.p.h.–miles per hour
o.j.–orange juice
P.S.–written after (post scriptum)
r.p.m.–revolutions per minute
r.s.v.p.–please reply (respondez s'il vous plaît)
t.v.–television
v.i.p.–very important person

Days of the Week

Sun., Sund.–Sunday
Mon.–Monday
Tues., Tu.–Tuesday
Wed.–Wednesday
Thurs., Thur., Th.–Thursday
Fri., Fr.–Friday
Sat.–Saturday

Months of the Year

Jan.–January
Feb.–February
Mar.–March
Apr.–April
Jul.–July
Aug.–August
Sept.–September
Oct.–October
Nov.–November
Dec.–December

Parts of Speech

adj.–adjective
adv.–adverb
conj.–conjunction
n.–noun
prep.–preposition
v.–verb

Name ____

TELL-A-PHONE ANSWERING SERVICE

Rewrite the telephone messages, using complete words in place of each abbreviation.

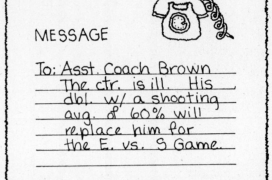

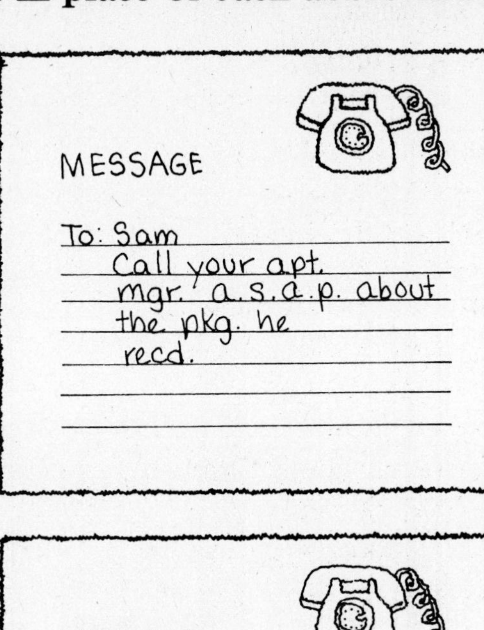
MESSAGE

To: Sam
Call your apt. mgr. a.s.a.p. about the pkg. he recd.

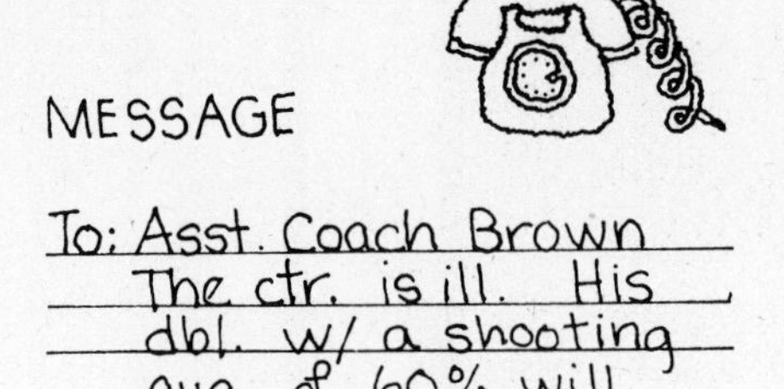
MESSAGE

To: Asst. Coach Brown
The ctr. is ill. His dbl. w/ a shooting avg. of 60% will replace him for the E. vs. S Game.

MESSAGE

To: Paul
Your ency. will be sent c.o.d. in c/o your atty.

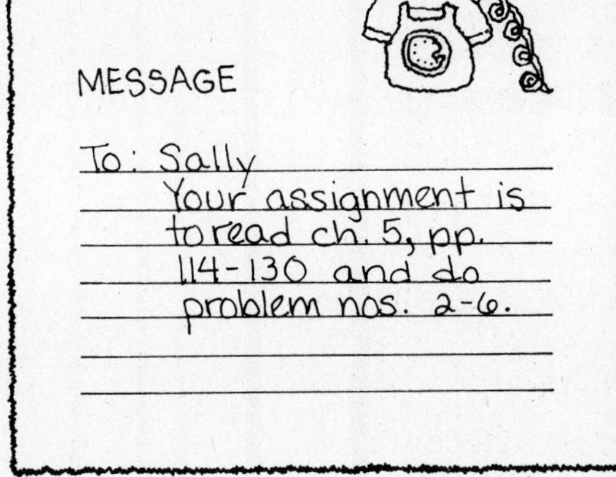
MESSAGE

To: Sally
Your assignment is to read ch. 5, pp. 114-130 and do problem nos. 2-6.

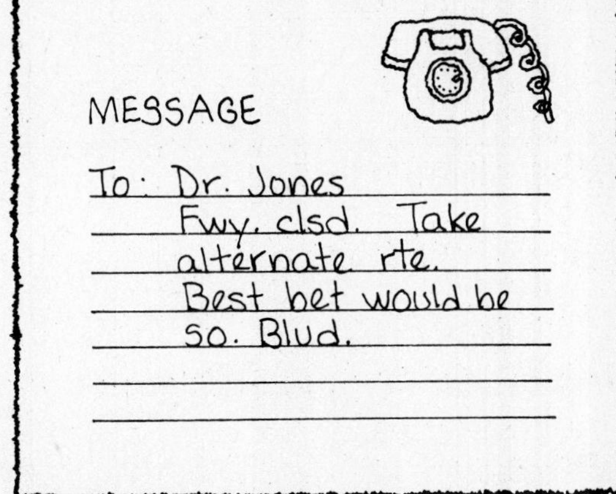
MESSAGE

To: Dr. Jones
Fwy. clsd. Take alternate rte. Best bet would be So. Blvd.

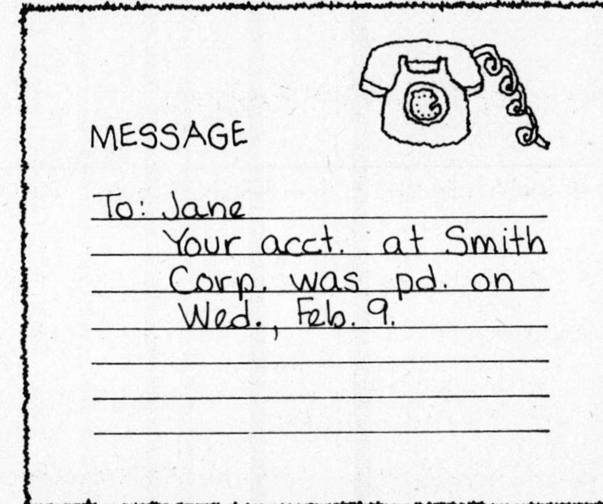
MESSAGE

To: Jane
Your acct. at Smith Corp. was pd. on Wed., Feb. 9.

SHORT FORMS

Here are some short forms often used as words.

awol–absent without leave
bems–bug-eyed monsters (sci-fi jargon)
biz–business
caps–capital letters
celebs–celebrities
chimp–chimpanzee
co-op–a cooperative
copter–helicopter
croc–crocodile
cuke–cucumber
deejay–disc jockey
deli–delicatessen
emcee–master or mistress of ceremonies
exam–examination
flu–influenza
gator–alligator
gym–gymnasium
hi fi–high fidelity
hippo–hippopotamus
home ec–home economics
hood–hoodlum
hose–hosiery
info–information

lab–laboratory
limo–limousine
lube–lubricate, lubrication
math–mathematics
mayo–mayonnaise
memo–memorandum
morn–morning
mums–chrysanthemums
peke–pekinese dog
photo–photograph
pix–pictures
pj's–pajamas
P.O.–Post Office
reps–representatives
rhino–rhinoceros
sarge–sergeant
sax–saxophone
sci fi–science fiction
sitcom–situation comedy
thru–through
tux–tuxedo
ump–umpire
vet–veteran, veterinarian
wiz–wizard

Activities With Short Forms

1. Write advertising slogans containing short forms for products or jobs.

   Hire a *limo* from Mr. Nimo.

   End each of your days
   in Smith's *P.J.*'s.

   For the answers to a quiz,
   go to see your local *wiz*.

2. Write sentences that contain several short forms.

   The *croc* and the *chimp* had *cukes* from the *deli*.

3. Fill in phrase patterns with a short-form word and a word that rhymes with it.

______________ of ______________

a ______________ ______________

the ______________ by a ______________

Examples of completed phrase patterns:

rows of hose

a large sarge

the ump by a dump

the chimp in a blimp

a cuke for a Duke

a cab with a lab

The completed phrases can be used:

a. as story titles;
b. as lines of poetry;
c. to make up silly questions;
d. to make silly stories by linking several phrases together.

CONTRACTIONS

aren't—are not
can't—cannot
couldn't—could not
didn't—did not
doesn't—does not
don't—do not
hadn't—had not
hasn't—has not
haven't—have not
isn't—is not
mightn't—might not
mustn't—must not
oughtn't—ought not
shouldn't—should not
wasn't—was not
weren't—were not
won't—will not
wouldn't—would not

I've—I have
they've—they have
you've—you have
we've—we have
he'd—he had, he would
I'd—I had, I would
she'd—she had, she would
they'd—they had, they would
we'd—we had, we would
you'd—you had, you would
we're—we are
you're—you are
there're—there are
they're—they are
I'm—I am
he's—he is, he has
it's—it is, it has

let's—let us
she's—she is, she has
that's—that is, that has
what's—what is, what has
where's—where is, where has
who's—who is, who has
I'll—I will, I shall
he'll—he will, he shall
it'll—it will, it shall
she'll—she will, she shall
they'll—they will, they shall
we'll—we will, we shall
who'll—who will, who shall
you'll—you will, you shall

PORTMANTEAUS

A portmanteau is a word formed by the arbitrary combination of two words. Lewis Carroll invented the portmanteaus *snark*, from snake and shark, and *slithy*, from slimy and lithe. Children can create their own portmanteaus from words on the Twins and Triplets List, page 39, or from familiar word pairs such as blue jeans, cottage cheese, and jump rope.

beefalo = beef + buffalo
bishaw = bicycle + rickshaw
botel = boat + hotel
broasted = broiled + roasted
brunch = breakfast + lunch

chortle = chuckle + snort

dumbfound = dumb + confound

eggler = egg + dealer
Eurasia = Europe + Asia

fantabulous = fantastic + fabulous
fishwich = fish + sandwich

galumphing = gallop + triumphing
guesstimate = guess + estimate

meld = melt + weld
mingy = mean + stingy
motel = motor + hotel
motorcade = motor car + cavalcade

smog = smoke + fog
splatter = splash + spatter
splotch = spot + blotch
splurge = splash + surge

vegeburger = vegetable + hamburger

three
SPELLING

SPELLING ODDS AND ENDS

These ten words appear in more than a quarter of all that we write:

the	a
and	in
of	that
to	you
I	for

Some words from a grade-school spelling book published in 1845:

cornucopiae	amanuensis
bacchanalian	circumambient
pusillanimity	

A 1950 article by Leslie W. Johnson cited these 5 words, from a list of 100, as most frequently misspelled by 14,643 children in the elementary grades.

their	they
too	then
there	

These 5 were the least often misspelled of the 100:

jumped
around
dropped
babies
money

The longest word in Webster's New Collegiate Dictionary, 8th edition:

pneumonoultramicroscopicsilicovolcanoconiosis

The longest word in the Oxford English Dictionary:

floccinaucinihilipilification

The first spelling book was printed in 1643 by Stephen Day in Cambridge, Massachusetts.

100 SPELLING DEMONS

ache
again
always
among
answer
any
been
beginning
believe
blue
break
built
business
busy
buy
can't
choose

color
coming
cough
could
country
dear
doctor
does
done
don't
early
easy
enough
every
February
forty
friend

grammar
guess
half
having
hear
heard
here
hoarse
hour
instead
just
knew
laid
loose
lose
making

many
meant
minute
much
none
often
once
piece
quiet
raise
read
ready
said
says
seems
separate

shoes
since
some
straight
sugar
sure
tear
their
there
they
though
through
tired
tonight
too
trouble
truly

Tuesday
two
used
very
wear
Wednesday
week
where
whether
which
whole
women
won't
would
write
writing
wrote

From W.F. Jones, *A Concrete Investigation of the Materials of English Spelling,* University Press: University of South Dakota, 1913.

243 ADDITIONAL SPELLING DEMONS

abrupt
absence
accommodate
accumulate
accurate
acquire
across
address
adequate
adjourn
advice
amateur
analysis

analyze
angle
apologize
apparently
appearance
appreciate
arctic
argument
arrangement
athletic
audience
before
benefited

bicycle
breathe
brilliant
bulletin
calendar
campaign
canceled
career
cemetery
certain
chief
colonel
column

committee
conscience
continuous
correspondence
courteous
criticism
curiosity
cylinder
decision
definitely
difference
different
difficulty

dining
disappear
disappoint
discipline
disease
dissatisfied
division
eighth
embarrass
environment
equipped
especially
etc.

exaggerate
excellent
existence
experience
extremely
familiar
fascinate
finally
foreign
formally
formerly
fulfill
fundamental
glimpse
gorgeous
government
governor
groceries
guarantee
guard
guidance
handsome
height
heroes
hoping
humorous
hurriedly
illegible
illustrate
imaginary
immediately
incidentally
independence
indispensable
intelligence
interesting
interpreted
interrupt
irrelevant
its
it's
jealous
jewelry
journey
judgment
khaki
kindergarten
knead
knowledge
laboratory
leisure
library
license
licorice
lightning
likely
listen
livelihood
loneliness
maintenance
maneuver
manufacture
marriage
mathematics
medicine
mileage
miniature
miscellaneous
mischievous
misspell
mortgage
muscle
naturally
necessary
nickel
niece
ninety
ninth
noticeable
nuisance
occasion
occur
occurred
o'clock
omission
omitted
opinion
opportunity
opposite
original
pamphlet
parallel
particular
pastime
peaceable
performance
permanent
personal
personnel
persuade
pleasant
possession
precede
privilege
probably
procedure
proceed
professor
pronunciation
psychology
pumpkin
pursue
quantity
quarrel
quite
realize
receive
recognize
recommend
rehearse
relevant
relief
relieve
religious
repetition
restaurant
rheumatism
rhubarb
rhythm
ridiculous
safety
schedule
scissors
seize
sergeant
severely
similar
sizable
souvenir
strength
studying
succeed
sufficient
surprise
temperature
temporary
tendency
therefore
thorough
together
tomorrow
tongue
transferred
typical
unanimous
undoubtedly
unique
unnecessary
until
usually
utensil
vacancy
vacuum
vegetable
vinegar
visible
volume
weather
wholly
who's
whose
yacht
yield
yolk
your
you're
youth
zealous

A SPELLING LIST FOR TEACHERS

accept
achievement
address
adequate
adjust
administrator
adolescents
affect
aggressive
algebra
alternative
anonymous
anxiety
applies
argument
arithmetic
assignment
assistant
attitude
audio-visual
behavior
bookkeeping
boundaries
building
business
cafeteria
calendar
Catholic
census
certain
channels
children
choir
climbing
commercial
community
comparative
complaints
compulsory
conference
coordinator
correspondence
corridor
counselor
courteous
criticism
curriculum
decision
deficient
delinquency
democratic
despite
destructive
detention
different
diploma
disastrous
discipline
discrimination
discussion
distraction
distribute
district
diverts
effect
elementary
entrance
epileptic
everything
excellent
exception
exercise
experiment
extension
faculty
field
foreign
genius
grammar
government
group
guidance
guilty
gymnasium
handicapped
hectic
height
heterogeneous
history
homogeneous
honorary
illiterate
immature
incidentally
independently
innocent
instructor
insurance
integration
intelligence
irate
irritated
janitor
journal
judgment
laid
languages
leisure
library
license
lounge
luncheon
Lutheran
mathematics
mischievous
motivated
municipal
necessary
negative
Negroes
observant
opportunities
orchestra
parental
parochial
perform
physics
pieces
plumbing
practically
practice
preference
prejudice
premises
preparatory
principal
professor
projector
psychiatric
quiet
quit
quite
receive
recess
recognize
reference
repetition
reprimand
requirements
responsible
salary
secondary
secretary
segregation
sensitive
significant
sincerely
smoking
sophomore
status
strength
student
suburban
successful
superintendent
supervisor
technology
tenure
theories
tried
truly
typical
ultimately
usually
vacancy
violent
vocational
(plus names of local businesses, streets, etc.)

Reprinted with permission from "When Teachers Misspell," *Improving College and University Teaching* (Spring, 1965). Corvallis, Ore.: Oregon State University Press.

FOR SYLLABIC SHOWOFFS

Most children love to impress family and friends by spelling long words or words with repetitive spelling patterns. Here's a list to show off with.

3 syllables	**4 syllables**	**5 syllables**	**6 syllables**
Chihuahua	Chattanooga	abracadabra	encyclopedia
committee	eucalyptus	auditorium	octogenarian
cucumber	gargantuan	bibliography	onomatopoeia
cumulus	gobbledegook	dieffenbachia	paleontology
discotheque	graduation	hippopotamus	
Frankenstein	harum-scarum	tonsillectomy	
labyrinth	hocus-pocus	whatchamacallit	
millionaire	independent	thingamadoodle	
	kookaburra		
	Minnehaha		
	Mississippi		
	Tallahassee		
	Transylvania		

12 syllables: antidisestablishmentarianism

14 syllables: supercalifragilisticexpialidocious

SPELLING PLURALS

Add *es* to words that end in *o* to make plurals.

buffalo*	motto*	embargo	torpedo
cargo*	potato	hero*	veto
domino*	tomato	mango*	volcano*
echo	tornado*		zero*

*These words add either *s* or *es*.

Add *es* to words that end in *s, ch, z, x,* or *sh* to make plurals.

ax	speech
buzz	splash
crush	tax
glass	topaz
guess	waltz
mash	watch
sandwich	wish

Change the *f* or *fe* to *v* before adding *es* to words that end in *f* or *fe* to make plurals.

calf	life	thief
half	loaf	wharf
knife	self	wife
leaf	shelf	wolf

Change the *y* to *i* before adding *es* to words that end in a consonant and *y* to make plurals.

ally
apply
army
baby
berry
body
city
copy
cry
fairy
fancy
fly
history
lady
lily
marry
mystery
reply
sky
spy
story
worry

IRREGULAR PLURALS

Singular	**Plural**
analysis	analyses
antenna	antennae
axis	axes
bacterium	bacteria
basis	bases
cactus	cactuses, cacti
child	children
crisis	crises
curriculum	curricula, curriculums
datum	data
die	dice
foot	feet
goose	geese
hippopotamus	hippopotamuses, hippopotami
man	men
medium	media
mouse	mice
nebula	nebulae
oasis	oases
ox	oxen
parenthesis	parentheses
phenomenon	phenomena
radius	radii
stratum	strata
tooth	teeth
woman	women

THE LAST WORD—NATIONAL SPELLING BEE WORDS

Here are the last words that have been spelled correctly by the winners of the National Spelling Bee since 1970.

croissant	1970
shalloon	1971
macerate	1972
vouchsafe	1973
hydrophyte	1974
incisor	1975
narcolepsy	1976
cambist	1977

Here are 18 other words on which the championships have been won or lost since the Spelling Bee began in 1926.

abbacy
acquiesced
asceticism
brethren
cinnabar
condominium
esquamulose
eudaemonic
gladiolus
larghetto
onerous
pronunciation
propitiatory
propylaeum
psychiatry
sacrilegious
transept
uncinated

WRITE IT RIGHT—HOMONYMS

acclamation, acclimation
adds, ads, adz
aerie, airy
ail, ale
air, ere, err, heir
aisle, I'll, isle
allowed, aloud
altar, alter
ate, eight
auger, augur
auricle, oracle

bail, bale
baize, bays
bald, balled, bawled
balm, bomb
band, banned
bare, bear
based, baste
beat, beet
beer, bier
bell, belle
better, bettor
blew, blue
bloc, block
boar, bore
boarder, border
bough, bow
bouillon, bullion
braise, brays, braze
bridal, bridle

cache, cash
capital, capitol
carat (karat), caret, carrot
cedar, ceder, seeder
cell, sell
cent, scent, sent
cense, cents, scents, sense
cereal, serial
cetaceous, setaceous
cheap, cheep
chews, choose
choler, collar
choral, coral
chorale, corral
chord, cord, cored
chute, shoot
cite, sight, site
clause, claws
coarse, course
coax, Cokes
colonel, kernel
core, corps
cue, queue
cymbal, symbol

dear, deer
dense, dents
descent, dissent
desert, dessert
dew, do, due
die, dye
doe, dough
ducked, duct

ewe, yew, you

faint, feint
fair, fare
faze, phase
feat, feet
fisher, fissure
flair, flare
flea, flee
flew, flu, flue
flocks, phlox
flour, flower
foaled, fold
for, fore, four
foul, fowl
frays, phrase
frees, freeze, frieze

gait, gate
gamble, gambol
genes, jeans
gilt, guilt
gneiss, nice
gnu, knew, new
gored, gourd
grate, great
grease, Greece
groan, grown
grocer, grosser
guessed, guest
guise, guys

hair, hare
hall, haul
handsome, hansom
hart, heart
hay, hey
heal, heel, he'll
hear, here
heard, herd
higher, hire
him, hymn
hoard, horde
hoarse, horse
hoes, hose
hole, whole
hour, our
humerus, humorous
idle, idol, idyll
in, inn
invade, inveighed
jam, jamb
jinks, jinx
kill, kiln
knave, nave
knead, need
knight, night
knit, nit
knows, noes, nose
lacks, lax
laps, lapse
leak, leek
lessen, lesson
levee, levy
links, lynx
load, lode, lowed

loan, lone
locks, lox
made, maid
magnate, magnet
mail, male
main, Maine, mane
marshall, martial
mean, mien
meat, meet, mete
might, mite
moose, mousse
muscle, mussel
oar, or, ore
one, won
paced, paste
packed, pact
pail, pale
pair, pare, pear
palate, palette, pallet
patience, patients
pause, paws
peace, piece
peal, peel
pearl, purl
pedal, peddle
peer, pier
plait, plate
pore, pour
praise, prays, preys
presence, presents
prince, prints
principal, principle
profit, prophet

quarts, quartz
rain, reign, rein
raise, raze
rapped, rapt, wrapped
read, red
read, reed
real, reel
right, rite, write
ring, wring
road, rode, rowed
roes, rose, rows
rote, wrote
rye, wry
sail, sale
scene, seen
seam, seem
seas, sees, seize
serf, surf
sew, so, sow
shear, sheer
side, sighed
sighs, size
sleight, slight
soar, sore
sole, soul
some, sum
staid, stayed
stair, stare
stake, steak
stationary, stationery
step, steppe
straight, strait

suede, swayed
suite, sweet
sundae, Sunday
tail, tale
taught, taut
team, teem
tear, tier
teas, tease, tees
their, there, they're
threw, through
throes, throws
thyme, time
tic, tick
to, too, two
toad, toed, towed
toe, tow
tracked, tract
undo, undue
vain, vane, vein
wade, weighed
waist, waste
waits, weights
war, wore
ware, wear
weak, week
wood, would
yoke, yolk

Name ______________________________

A HOMONYM GIFT LIST

Directions: Write in a homonym for the underlined word and the name or kind of person who might get the gift.

1. a new boat sail on *sale* for Captain Hornblower
2. a ____________ donut with a *hole* for ____________
3. a pretty ____________ and a bag of *flour* for ____________
4. *hoes* and a ____________ for ____________
5. a night at the ____________ *in* Washington, D.C. for ____________
6. every *Sunday*, an ice cream ____________ for ____________
7. a new *red* book that can be easily ____________ for ____________
8. a ____________ of music would bring *peace* to ____________
9. a ____________ of paint in a *pale* color for ____________
10. *wood* ____________ be good for ____________
11. a fishing *reel* made of ____________ steel for ____________
12. a ____________ about the monkey's *tail* for ____________
13. the *right* kind of pen to ____________ with for ____________
14. a sweet-smelling ____________ to be *sent* to ____________
15. a ____________ of knives to *pare* a *pear* for ____________

four
PUT IT IN WRITING

72 different words

WORDS USED INSTEAD OF "SAID"

More Common

added
admitted
answered
argued
asked
babbled
bawled
bet
blurted
bragged
bugged
called
cautioned
chatted
cheered
chuckled
coaxed
confessed
corrected
cried
croaked
crowed
dared
decided
declared
demanded
denied
ended
exclaimed
explained
fretted
gasped
greeted
hinted
informed
insisted
laughed
lied
murmured
muttered
named
nodded
nudged
offered
ordered
panted
pleaded
praised
prayed
promised
questioned
quoted
ranted
reminded
replied
requested
roared
sassed
sighed
smiled
smirked
snickered
stammered
stated
stuttered
suggested
tempted
wailed
wept
whispered
wondered
yelled

Less Common

admonished
assented
atoned
bantered
bemoaned
berated
broached
cajoled
carped
challenged
cited
claimed
conceded
demurred
denounced
disclosed
drawled
droned
enjoined
enumerated
espoused
estimated
evinced
indicated
jeered
jested
lamented
leered
mocked
needled
opined
outlined
presented
proffered
projected
quibbled
quipped
quizzed
rebuked
rejoiced
renounced
retorted
revealed
scowled
simpered
speculated
sputtered
squelched
stipulated
stormed
theorized
vocalized
volunteered

Activities With "Said" Words

1. To comic strip bubbles, add:
    1) the name of the person speaking
    2) a word from the *said* list to show how the person is speaking
    3) any needed punctuation

2. Make a matching game of statements and words for *said.*

3. Categorize words with similar meanings into groups titled *pleading, anger, laughing, crying, asking,* and *answering.*
4. Write a song title or lyric. Add a phrase to show how it might be said. For example: *"Tie a yellow ribbon 'round the old elm tree,"* reminded Tony.
5. Add adverbs or phrases to words used instead of said to elaborate on how something is being spoken:

whispered softly — breathlessly gasped
whispered a little too loudly — gasped in a terrified way

Name ______________________________

CARTOON CAPTIONS

Write a caption for each picture. For each caption choose a statement from column A and a word from column B that tells how the statement is being said. Be sure to punctuate the captions you write.

"Give me some water," gasped the flower.	______ the chair.
______ the menu.	______ the soda pop.
______ the calculator.	______ the onion.
______ the dictionary.	______ the hamburger.
______ the telephone.	______ the refrigerator.

A	B
Don't forget to close the door	cried
I guess I'll have a straw	decided
Won't you have a seat	corrected
Have a bite	called
Don't cut me with that knife	tempted
Your spelling is wrong	ordered
I'll have a steak, potato, and a salad	reminded
Answer me when I ring	invited
Also, two plus two makes four	added

WORDS FOR RUN/WALK, LAUGH/CRY, SAD/HAPPY

Here are some alternatives for six words overused by children in their stories. Children can look them up and discuss the subtle differences between the words, and use them in the writing or editing of their stories.

Run	Walk	Laugh	Cry	Sad	Happy
bolt	amble	cackle	bawl	cheerless	blissful
chase	ambulate	chortle	blubber	crestfallen	blithe
dart	lumber	chuckle	howl	dejected	cheerful
dash	meander	crow	moan	depressed	delighted
flee	pace	giggle	sniffle	despondent	ecstatic
gallop	plod	grin	snivel	disheartened	elated
hurry	prance	guffaw	sob	dismal	exultant
jog	ramble	hoot	wail	dispirited	gay
lope	saunter	howl	weep	downcast	glad
race	shuffle	roar	whimper	downhearted	gleeful
rush	stagger	smile	whine	forlorn	jolly
scamper	step	snicker		joyless	jovial
scoot	stride	titter		melancholy	joyful
scramble	stroll			miserable	jubilant
scurry	strut			mournful	lighthearted
scuttle	swagger			pitiable	mirthful
speed	totter			sorrowful	overjoyed
sprint	trek			sorry	sunny
tear	trudge			unhappy	thrilled
trot				woebegone	tickled
				woeful	
				wretched	

SIMILES

Here are some similes that are as old as the hills, and activities to stimulate the writing of new ones.

as big as a house
as black as coal
as blind as a bat
as brown as a berry
as busy as a bee
as clean as a whistle
as clear as crystal
as cool as a cucumber
as easy as pie
as flat as a pancake
as fresh as a daisy
as good as gold
as happy as a lark
as hard as a rock
as light as a feather
as limp as a wet noodle
as mad as a hornet
as meek as a lamb
as neat as a pin
as pale as a ghost
as playful as a kitten
as pretty as a picture
as quick as a wink
as quiet as a mouse
as red as a beet
as sharp as a tack
as sick as a dog
as slippery as an eel
as slow as molasses
as sly as a fox
as smooth as silk
as stiff as a board
as straight as an arrow
as stubborn as a mule
as warm as toast
as white as a sheet
as wise as an owl

Activities With Similes

1. Make up new similes for the same descriptive adjectives as some of the examples on the list. *Example:* as big as a mountain
2. Make up similes that are completed by phrases.
as slippery as a newly polished dance floor
as easy as turning on the tap
3. Make up some comical similes to communicate the opposite meaning of an adjective. *Examples:*
"As clear as mud" means something was not clear at all.
as heavy as a bag of marshmallows
as pretty as Frankenstein's mother
4. Make up groups of similes.
similes for color words: as purple as a royal robe
similes that use animals as the basis of comparison: as jumpy as a kangaroo
similes for feeling words: as sad as the kittens who lost their mittens
similes that name famous people: as tall as Wilt Chamberlain
similes that are alliterative: as slow as a sloth; as rigid as a robot
5. Make up similes using the word "like."
A tree is like a chemical factory.
The catsup oozed across the hamburger like lava trailing down the side of the volcano.

Name ____________________

SIMILE FACTORY

Directions: Take the words through the Simile Factory. Complete each simile according to the directions on each machine.

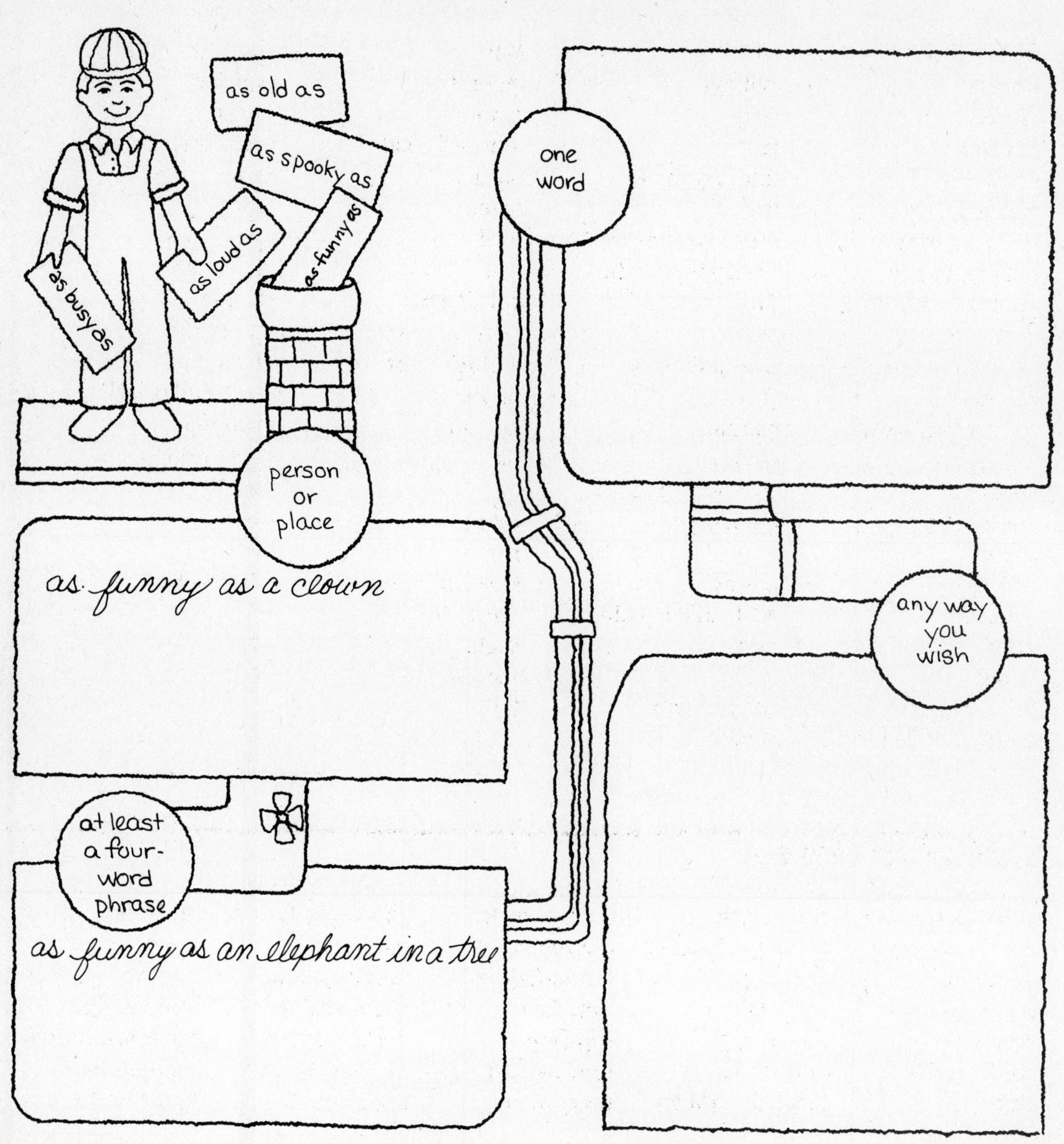

GOOD VS. EVIL WORDS

Superstition, magic, mystery, and spooky tales have great appeal for children of all ages. These Good vs. Evil Words can be used to stimulate discussion, research, and story writing.

abracadabra
amulet
banshee
bewitch
black cat
Blarney Stone
bride's garter
broken mirror
bubbles on coffee
buckeye
Ceres
charms
copper bracelet, anklet
cross
cross your fingers
cures
curse
demon
devil
Druid
Dryad
dwarf
elf
evil eye
fairy
fear
find a penny
fire
four-leaf clover
Friday the 13th
fungi
genie
Gesundheit
ghost
gnome
goblin
ground-hog day
horseshoe
imp
knock on wood
walk under ladder
Leo
luck
lycanthropy
Magi
Mars
mascot
moon
mustard seed
occult
omen
opal
Pan
poltergeist
Puck
rabbit's foot
rainbow
rat tail
rice
rites
robin
ruby
seventh child
signs
snake
sneezing
Sol
soul
spilling salt
spirits
stars
step on a crack
stub your toe
sun
taboo
toad
totem
triangle
troll
two-dollar bill
voodoo
werewolf
witch
zaps
Zeus
Zodiac
#7
#13
#3

FLIP-FLOP WORDS

abba-dabba
bibble-babble
boo-hoo
boogie-woogie
bow-wow
chiller-diller
chit-chat
click-clack
clickety-clackety
clip-clop
dilly-dally
ding-a-ling
ding-dong
dribble-drabble
ducky-wucky
even-Steven
fiddle-faddle
flim-flam
flip-flop
fuddy-duddy
fuzzy-wuzzy
giggle-gaggle
hanky-panky
harum-scarum
heebie-jeebies
helter-skelter
hippety-hoppety
hocus-pocus
hoity-toity
hokey-pokey
hootchie-cootchie
hully-gully
humpty-dumpty
hurdy-gurdy
hurly-burly

itsy-bitsy
jibber-jabber
jingle-jangle
lovey-dovey
mish-mash
mumbo-jumbo
namby-pamby
okey-dokey
palsy-walsy
piggly-wiggly
piggy-wiggy
ping-pong
pitter-patter
plip-plop
raggle-taggle
razzle-dazzle
rinky-dinky
rowdy-dowdy
rub-dub
scribble-scrabble
see-saw
shilly-shally
splish-splash
super-duper
teeny-weeny
teensy-weensy
tick-tock
ticky-tacky
tip-top
tippety-toppety
tootsie-wootsie
trip-trap
walkie-talkie
whing-ding
wibble-wobble
wig-wag
wiggle-waggle
willy-nilly
wishy-washy
yakety-yak
zig-zag

Activities With Flip-Flop Words

1. Choose several flip-flop words. Write short stories in which the flip-flop words repeat themselves, or appear in a pattern, such as in Rikki-Tikki-Tembo or The Three Billy Goats Gruff.
2. Find flip-flop words that name sounds. Use the words to represent sounds in sentences.

   "Trip-trap, trip-trap" went the boots on the bridge.

   The "click-clack" of the crickets became softer at dawn.
3. Make up story titles that include a flip-flop word and another word that is related by sound or meaning.

   The Wishy-Washy Laundry

   The Jibber-Jabber Gypsies

   The Super-Duper Blooper

SECRET WRITING—CODES AND CIPHERS

Spacing Code

A super-simple position code is made by merely changing the position of the spaces between words.

DANGEROUS TO REMAIN LEAVE AT ONCE
DA NGERO USTOR EMAI NLEA VEATO NCE

Every Other Letter Cipher

This is a very simple cipher, in which random letters are inserted between each letter of the actual message, and then all the letters are grouped into "words" of five letters each. The cipher begins with a random letter. Meaningless letters may be added to the last "word" to complete the five-letter pattern. The message SECRET MEETING AT BLACK LAGOON would look something like this, depending on the random letters selected:

TSREF CLRNE QTXMS ELERT PIKNR GVAMT NBOLR ADCEK MLPAG GIOLO SNRTU

Double Parallel-Alphabet Cipher

Select a key word of at least seven letters that does not use the same letter twice. Following it, write the alphabet omitting any letter found within the key word. Now write the alphabet beneath this.

G E R M A N Y B C D F H I J K L O P Q S T U V W X Z
A B C D E F G H I J K L M N O P Q R S T U V W X Y Z

The message WATCH OUT, becomes VGSRB KTS using this cipher.

Alphabet Strips

Write the alphabet with an even space between each letter on a strip of paper. Now, on a longer strip, write the alphabet twice, again with an even space between each letter. A letter is agreed upon as the code name. Place the shorter strip above this letter on the longer strip. Then write the message in letters from the lower strip. Here is the set-up for a "D" code.

A B C D E F G H I J K L M N O P Q R S T U V W X Y Z

A B C D E F G H I J K L M N O P Q R S T U V W X Y Z A B C D E F

Here is a "D" code message: SODB LW VDIH

Chinese Cipher

The Chinese Cipher is a simple transposition cipher in which the letters of the message are written up and down columns, beginning in the upper right-hand corner.* MEET ME AT THE SHIP AT MIDNIGHT would first be written in columns like this:

N D E H M
I I S T E
G M H T E
H T I A T
T A P E M

The coded message would then be written: NDEHM IISTE GMHTE HTIAT TAPEM

*Meaningless letters may be added to the columns to complete the pattern.

Bacon's Cipher

Francis Bacon, the English philosopher and author, invented this cipher which uses only two letters of the alphabet (a and b) in various combinations.

A	aaaaa	N	abbaa
B	aaaab	O	abbab
C	aaaba	P	abbba
D	aaabb	Q	abbbb
E	aabaa	R	baaaa
F	aabab	S	baaab
G	aabba	T	baaba
H	aabbb	UV	baabb
IJ	abaaa	W	babaa
K	abaab	X	babab
L	ababa	Y	babba
M	ababb	Z	babbb

Using this cipher, URGENT would read:

baabbbaaaaaabbaaabaaabbaabaaba

Tic Tac Toe Cipher

The letters of the alphabet are first arranged in a diagram.

AB	CD	EF
GH	IJ	KL
MN	OP	QR

For the first letter of any pair, draw that part of the diagram. For the second letter of any pair, draw that part of the diagram, and add a dot. For example,

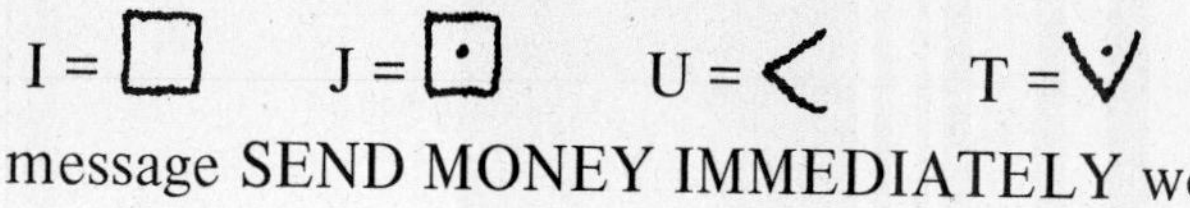

The message SEND MONEY IMMEDIATELY would be written:

DECODEABLE STATE MOTTOES

These state mottoes can be decoded using the codes on pages 62-64.

Spacing Code:
LIB ERTYA NDUN IONN OWA NDFO REVE RONEA NDINS EPA RAB LE

Every Other Letter Cipher:
FAPLO LSFTO XRUOY UPRMC DOPUG NHTAR LYSOT

Double Parallel Alphabet Cipher:
SBA HGQS NPKJSCAP

Alphabet Strip in "D" code:
OLEHUWB DQG SURVSHULWB

Chinese Cipher:
EDYTV NNARI CENER EPDBT OEIIU SDNLE

Bacon's Cipher:
aabaababababaaabaaabaaababababaaababaaaabbabbaaaaaabbbabaaaaabbaaabbbaabaabaaaa

Tic Tac Toe Cipher:

CODEABLE STATE MOTTOES AND NICKNAMES

Alabama	Audemus jura nostra defendere We dare to defend our rights Cotton state
Alaska	North to the future The last frontier
Arizona	Ditat Deus God enriches Grand Canyon state
Arkansas	Regnat populus The people rule; Land of opportunity Wonder state
California	Eureka I've found it Golden state

Colorado	Nil sine numine
	Nothing without the deity
	Centennial state
Connecticut	Qui transtulit sustinet
	He who transplanted continues to sustain
	Constitution state, Nutmeg state
Delaware	Liberty and Independence
	Diamond state, Blue Hen state, First state
Florida	In God we trust
	Peninsula state, Sunshine state
Georgia	Wisdom, justice, moderation
	Empire State of the South, Peach state
Hawaii	Ua mau ke ea o ka aina i ka pono
	The life of the land is perpetuated in righteousness
	Aloha state
Idaho	Esto perpetua
	Mayest thou endure forever
	Gem state
Illinois	State, sovereignty, national union
	Prairie state, Sucker state, Inland Empire
Indiana	The crossroads of America
	Hoosier state
Iowa	Our liberties we prize, and rights we maintain
	Hawkeye state
Kansas	Ad astra per aspera
	To the stars through difficulties
	Sunflower state, Jayhawker state
Kentucky	United we stand, divided we fall
	Blue grass state, Corncracker state
Louisiana	Union, justice, and confidence
	Pelican state, Creole state
Maine	Dirigo
	I guide
	Pine Tree state
Maryland	Scuto bonae voluntatis tuae coronasti nos
	With the shield of thy goodwill thou hast covered us
	Old-Line state, Free state
Massachusetts	Ense petit placidam sub libertate quietem
	By the sword we seek peace, but peace only under liberty
	Bay state, Old Colony state

Michigan	Si quaeris peninsulam amoenam circumspice If you seek a pleasant peninsula, look around you Wolverine state, Great Lake state
Minnesota	L'étoile du nord The star of the north Gopher state, North Star state
Mississippi	Virtute et armis By valor and arms Bayou state, Magnolia state
Missouri	Salus populi suprema lex esto Let the welfare of the people be the supreme law Show Me state
Montana	Oro y plata Gold and silver Treasure state
Nebraska	Equality before the law Cornhusker state, Tree Planter state
Nevada	All for our country Sagebrush state, Silver state
New Hampshire	Live free or die Granite state
New Jersey	Liberty and prosperity Garden state
New Mexico	Crescit eundo It grows as it goes Sunshine state, Land of Enchantment
New York	Excelsior Higher Empire state
North Carolina	Esse quam videri To be rather than to seem Tarheel state, Turpentine state
North Dakota	Liberty and union, now and forever, one and inseparable Sioux state, Flickertail state
Ohio	With God, all things are possible Buckeye state
Oklahoma	Labor omnia vincit Labor conquers all things Sooner state
Oregon	The union Beaver state

Pennsylvania	Virtue, liberty, and independence
	Keystone state
Rhode Island	Hope
	Little Rhody state
South Carolina	Animis opibusque parati
	Ready in soul and resource
	Palmetto state
South Dakota	Under God the people rule
	Coyote state
Tennessee	Agriculture and commerce
	Volunteer state
Texas	Friendship
	Lone Star state
Utah	Industry
	Beehive state
Vermont	Freedom and unity
	Green Mountain state
Virginia	Sic semper tyrannis
	Thus ever to tyrants
	Old Dominion state
Washington	Alki
	By and by
	Evergreen state
West Virginia	Montani semper liberi
	Mountaineers are always free men
	Mountain state
Wisconsin	Forward
	Badger state
Wyoming	Cedant arma togae
	Let arms yield to the gown
	Equality state

LETTER-WRITING ADDRESSES

Here's a list of addresses to give children so that they can write real letters to real places and people, and wait for real replies.

Baseball Commissioner's Office
75 Rockefeller Plaza
New York, New York 10019

National League Office (baseball)
Mills Building
220 Montgomery Street
San Francisco, California 94104

American League Office (baseball)
280 Park Avenue
New York, New York 10017

National Hockey League Headquarters
920 Sun Life Building
Montreal, Quebec H3B 2W2

National Basketball Association
League Office
2 Pennsylvania Plaza, Suite 2010
New York, New York 10001

National Football League Office
410 Park Avenue
New York, New York 10022

NASA
Lyndon B. Johnson Space Center
Houston, Texas 77058

World Wildlife Fund
Suite 728
910 - 17th Street N.W.
Washington, D.C. 20036

National Audubon Society
1130 5th Avenue
New York, New York 10028

International Frisbee Association
P.O. Box 4578
North Hollywood, California 91607

Circus Fans Association of America
P.O. Box 605
Aurora, Illinois 60507

National Dairy Council
6300 North River Road
Rosemont, Illinois 60018

National Hot Rod Association
10639 Riverside Drive
North Hollywood, California 91602

Society of American Magicians
66 Marked Tree Road
Needham, Massachusetts 02192

National Model Railroad Association
7061 Twin Oaks Drive
Indianapolis, Indiana 46226

American Numismatic Association
818 North Cascade
Colorado Springs, Colorado 80903

U.S. Table Tennis Association
Box 815
Orange, Connecticut 06477

National Investigations Committee
on Unidentified Flying Objects
7970 Woodman Avenue
Van Nuys, California 91402

International Kitefliers Association
c/o Mr. Will Yolen
321 East 48th Street
New York, New York 10017

Bureau of Consumer Protection
Federal Trade Commission
Washington, D.C. 20580

IUCN (International Union for the
Conservation of Nature)
1110 Morges
Switzerland

Walt Disney Productions
500 South Buena Vista Street
Burbank, California 91521

NBC-TV
3000 West Alameda Avenue
Burbank, California 91505
or
30 Rockefeller Plaza
New York, New York 10020

International Friendship League, Inc.
(pen-pals)
40 Mount Vernon Street
Boston, Massachusetts 02108

Common Cause
2030 M Street, N.W.
Washington, D.C. 20036

CBS Television
7800 Beverly Boulevard
Los Angeles, California 90036

REBUS WORDS

Whenever block letters appear in the following words, the letter name is pronounced; whereas sounds are to be pronounced for lower case letters. For example,  TTTT for tease and 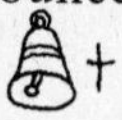 + for belt.

are  R

ate  8

be 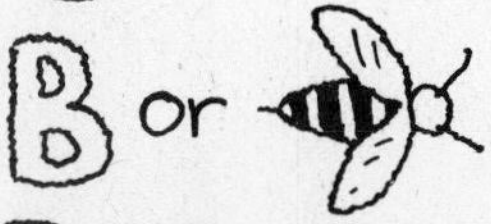 B or

beautiful  BUTful

beauty  BUT

bee  B

bees  BBBB

before 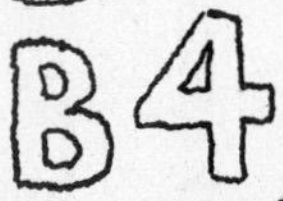 B4

belief  B

belly E

belt +

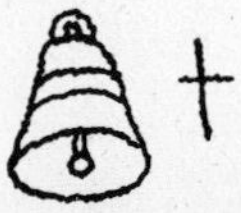

boat +

can  SOUP

cartoon

cookie  E

delight  D

eerie  E

elbow  L

fancy 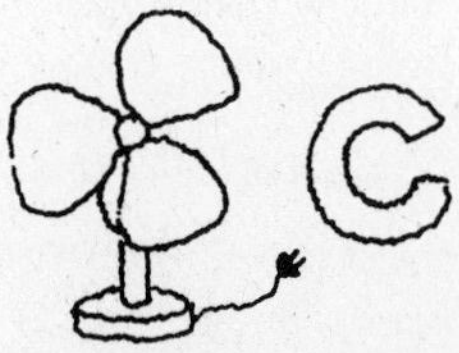 C

for  4

glasses  or

handy 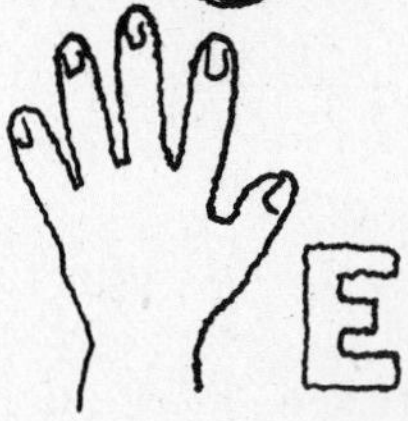 E

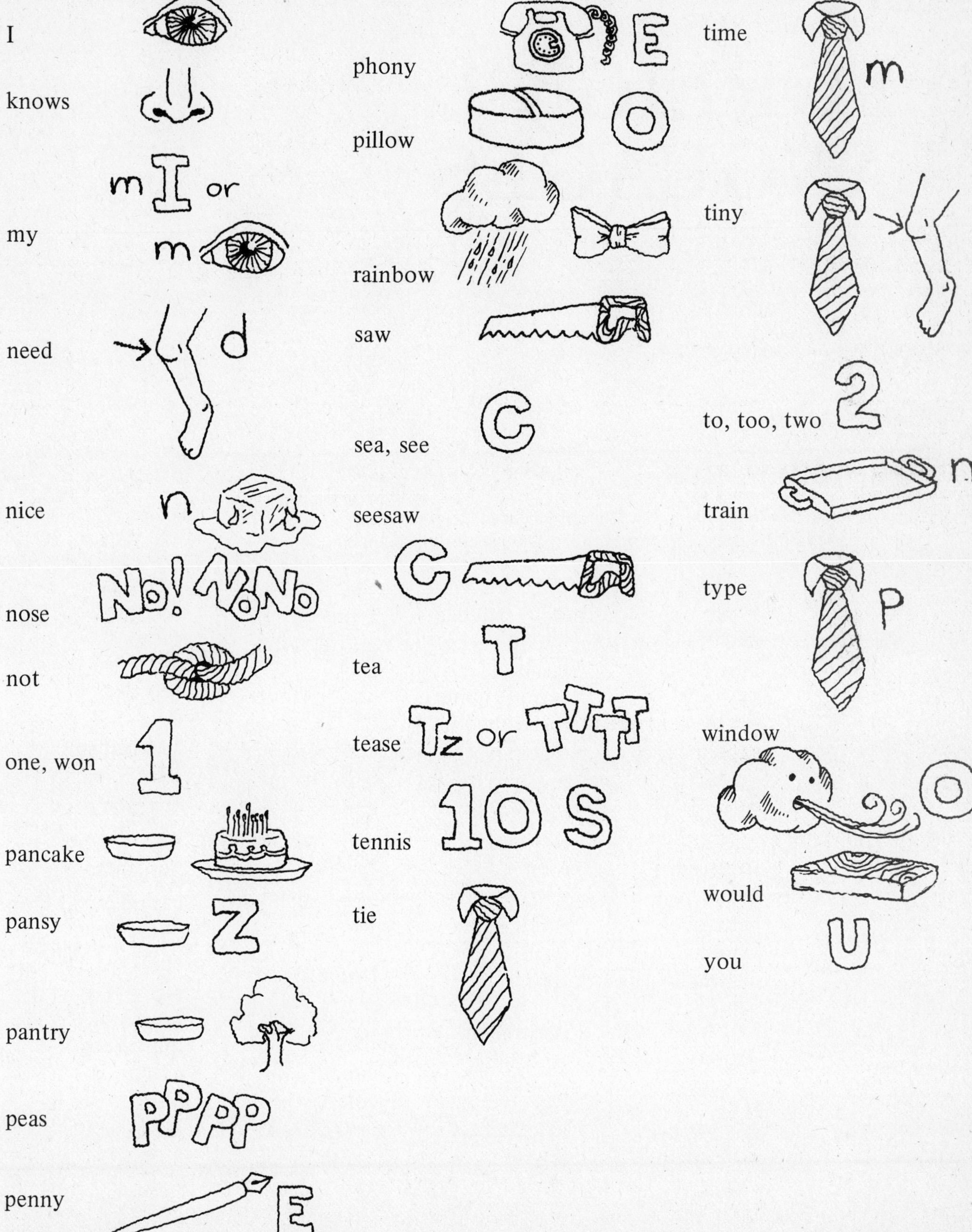
I
knows
my
or
need
nice
nose
not
one, won
pancake
pansy
pantry
peas
penny
phony
pillow
rainbow
saw
sea, see
seesaw
tea
tease
or
tennis
tie
time
tiny
to, too, two
train
type
window
would
you

five

"FOREIGN" LANGUAGES

BORROWED WORDS

We have adopted the following words from other languages with only some minor spelling changes. Sometimes the original spelling will appear for its interest value.

African

goober
gumbo
okra
tote
voodoo
yam
zombie

American Indian

canoe
caucus
chipmunk
hickory
(pohickery)
hominy
mackinaw
moccasin
moose
opossum
papoose
pecan
persimmon
powwow
raccoon
skunk (segongw)
squash
squaw
succotash
(msiquatash)
toboggan
tomahawk
totem
wampum
wigwam

Arabic

alcohol
algebra
azimuth
caliph
fakir
genie (jinnī)
harem
hashish
lemon (limun)
magazine
mattress
mufti
muslim
rubaiyat
sahib
sherbet
sofa
tariff
zero

Australian Aborigine

boomerang
kangaroo
kiwi
koala
wombat

Basque

jai alai

Chinese

chop suey
chow mein
gung ho
ketchup
kowtow
kumquat
tea

Dutch

brandy
Bronx
clipper
coleslaw
(kool sla)
cruise
gin
Harlem
schooner
sloop
waffle (wafel)
Yonkers

East Indian (Hindi, Sanskrit)

bandana
bungalow
cashmere
cheetah
chintz
chutney
dinghy
dungarees
gunny
guru
jute
karma
loot
madras

polo
pundit
rajah
shampoo
swami
yoga

Egyptian

gum
pharaoh

Eskimo

caribou
kayak

French

amour
au gratin
avant-garde
beret
bistro
bonbon
bourbon
cadet
cadre
café
camaraderie
camouflage
carafe
cartel
champagne
chef
chiffon
cliché
clique
collage
commune
corsage
crêpe
crevasse
critique
crochet
croutons
decor
enclave
entrée
foyer
fuselage
garage
lecture
levee
litre
mademoiselle
masseur
montage
motif
naiveté
parfait
parole
partisan
pastel
penchant
portage
purée
rapport
reprise
revue
ricochet
rouge
roulette
sabotage
saboteur
sauté
savant
suite
timbre
toupee
vignette

German

blitzkrieg
cobalt
dachshund
delicatessen
dumb
edelweiss
fahrenheit
frau
fraulein
hamburger
herr
kaiser
kindergarten
leitmotiv
limburger
loafer
nickel
noodle
poodle
pretzel
pumpernickel
putsch
quartz
riesling
sauerkraut
schnapps
schnitzel
Volkswagen
waltz
wurst

Greek

asphasia
aura
circus
dialect
diaspora
dogma
eureka
genesis
nausea
paranoia
phobia
psyche
psychosis
schema

Haitian

barbecue
(barbacoa)
cassava
manioc

Hebrew

amen
cinnamon
(qinnamon)
hallelujah
jubilee
kibbutz
messiah
rabbi
shalom

Hungarian

coach
goulash
hussar
paprika

Italian

allegro
andante
balcony
balloon
bandit
baroque
bravo
broccoli
cacciatore
cadenza
cameo
cantata
fiasco
fresco
madonna
minestrone
oratorio
pasta
pianissimo
pilot
portico
prima donna
regatta
replica
salvo
sirocco
soprano
staccato
studio
trombone
vibrato
violin

Japanese

geisha
haiku
ju-jitsu
kabuki
kimono
nisei
rickshaw
samurai
soy
tempura
teriyaki
tycoon

Latin

abacus
ad hoc
alias
alibi
alma mater
alumnus
auditor
axis
bacillus
calculus
campus
cancer
dictum
etcetera
extra
forum
fungus
gratis
humus
integer
juxta
per diem
per se
pro rata
quantum
quid pro quo
ratio
recipe
regalia
rostrum
solitaire
spatula
subpoena
symposium
tabula rasa
tibia
toga
trivia
ultra

Malay

amuck
bamboo
caddy
cockatoo
gingham
gong
mango
paddy
sarong

Persian

bazaar
caravan
divan
mogul
shah
shawl

Polish

polka

Polynesian

taboo
tattoo
ukulele

Portuguese

albino
fetish
marmalade
molasses

Russian

intelligentsia
kremlin
pogrom
samovar
steppe
tundra
vodka

Scandinavian

egg
fiord
ill
saga
ski
skin
skirt
smorgasbord

South American Indian

quinine
tapioca
tapir

Spanish

adobe
amigo
banana
bolero
bonanza
bronco
burro
caballero
canyon
chili
cocoa
corral
coyote
fiesta
gaucho
gringo
hombre
junta
lariat
machete
macho
mariachi
marimba
mesa
mesquite
mustang
padre
paella
palomino
patio
plaza
poncho
pueblo
rodeo
señor
sierra
simpatico
sombrero
stampede
tamale
tomato
tortilla
vigilante

Yiddish

bagel
blintzes
chutzpah
kibitzer
kosher
nosh
schlemiel
schlepp
schmaltz

Activities With Borrowed Words

1. Categorize words into groups, such as foods, people, clothing, animals, furniture, objects, places, verbs, and adjectives. Do you notice a certain pattern in the types of words we've borrowed from each language?
2. Draw a word origins world map.
3. Make up a story using as many borrowed words as you can.

   Herr Schmidt's *broccoli ricocheted* across the *fiord* and landed in *Mademoiselle's foyer* on top of her *moccasins.*

4. Use the library and dictionaries to trace the origin and development of several borrowed words.
5. Make up analogies using several of the borrowed words.

   Moccasin is to feet as *beret* is to head; *garage* is to *Volkswagen* as *corral* is to *bronco.*

6. Look up borrowed words in a dictionary that lists word etymologies and show the word's spelling and meaning in the original language.

   magazine = makhazin (Arabic)–a storehouse
   sherbet = sharbah (Arabic)–a cool drink
   ketchup = ke-tsiap (Chinese)–a brine from pickled fish, used as a sauce

BORROWED PHRASES

French

à la carte–meal dishes separately priced
au contraire–on the contrary
au courant–up to date
au naturel–in a natural state
au revoir–goodbye
bête noir–pet aversion
bon voyage–have a good journey
cause célèbre–situation arousing attention; noted incident
c'est la vie–that's life
cherchez la femme–a woman caused it: look for the woman

coup de grâce—final, decisive action
coup d'état—a sudden change in government, often caused by force
creme de la crème—the very best
de rigeur—indispensable; required by fashion or custom
double entendre—double meaning
en masse—as a group
fait accompli—an accomplished and irrevocable fact or action
faux pas—a social error
hors d'ouevre—appetizer
joie de vivre—zest or enthusiasm for the pleasures of life
laissez faire—policy of noninterference
nom de plume—pen name
nouveau riche—newly or recently rich
par excellence—of highest quality
pièce de resistance—major or chief item of a series
raison d'être—reason for being
sans souci—without worry
savoir faire—sophistication; know-how
tour de force—feat of strength or brilliance
vis-à-vis—face to face; in relation to

German

auf Wiedersehen—till we meet again

Greek

hoi polloi—the general mass of people

Latin

ad hoc—for the present situation; temporary
ad infinitum—without limit
ad nauseam—to the point of disgust
alter ego—one's other self; a confidential friend
bona fide—sincere; genuine
caveat emptor—let the buyer beware
ex post facto—after the fact, retroactive
in extremis—near death
in toto—entirely
mea culpa—I'm guilty

modus operandi–method of operation
non sequitur–illogical; conclusion that does not follow from the evidence
persona non grata–an unwelcome or unacceptable person
rara avis–an unusual person or thing
status quo–the situation as is, without change
sub rosa–privately; secretly
tempus fugit–time flies
vox populi–the voice of the people

Spanish

Quien sabe?–Who knows?
Vaya con Dios–May God be with you

IGPAY ATINLAY AND OTHER SECRET LANGUAGES

Although examples have been given in writing, all of these secret languages are meant to be spoken, not written.

Pig Latin

To speak Pig Latin, take the first letter or the consonant blend from the beginning of a word, put it at the end of the word and add the sound *ay* to it. To all words beginning with a vowel, leave the word as is and add *way* to the end of it.
Jack and Jill went up the hill becomes:

ACKJAY ANDWAY ILLJAY ENTWAY UPWAY ETHAY ILLHAY

Na and Gree

To speak Na or Gree add *na* or *gree* to the end of each word.

JACKNA ANDNA JILLNA WENTNA UPNA THENA HILLNA
or JACKGREE ANDGREE JILLGREE WENTGREE UPGREE THEGREE HILLGREE

Skimono Jive

To speak Skimono Jive, add *sk* to the beginning of each word.

SKJACK SKAND SKJILL SKWENT SKUP SKTHE SKHILL

Ong

To speak ong, add *ong* before every vowel sound.

JONGACK ONGAND JONGILL WONGENT ONGUP THONGE HONGILL

Pelf Latin or Alfalfa

To speak Pelf or Alfalfa insert *lf* after every vowel sound and then repeat the vowel sound.
JALFACK ALFAND JILFILL WELFENT ULFUP THELFE HILFILL

G or Goose Language

To speak G or Goose Language insert a *g* after the beginning sound in each syllable.
JGACK AGND JGILL WGENT UGP THGE HGILL
This might sound something like this:
Juhgack′agand′juhgill′wegent′uhgup′thuhguh′higill′

COCKNEY RHYMING SLANG

Rhyming slang became highly developed among the thieves of early- to mid-nineteenth-century London. Using it helped keep secrets from outsiders who might overhear a conversation. Although rhyming slang later spread to Australia, it is still generally known as Cockney Rhyming Slang.

alone–Pat Malone
arm–false alarm
bed–Uncle Ned
boots–daisy roots
bread–strike me dead
butter–roll me in the gutter
cake–give and take
cheese–balmy breeze, cough and sneeze, or stand at ease
coat–I'm afloat
corner–Johnny Horner
crook–babbling brook
cupboard–Mother Hubbard
dead–brown bread
dinner–Lilley and Skinner
dollar–Oxford scholar
ears–butter and beers
face–chevy chase
feet–plates o' meat
finger–lean and linger
flowers–happy half-hours
girl–twist and twirl
good–Robin Hood
hands–German bands
hat–lean and fat or tit for tat
head–loaf of bread or lump of lead
husband (old man)–pot and pan
I–mince pie
jail–jug and pail
knees–two's and three's
mate–china plate
Missus–cows and kisses
money–bees and honey or sugar and honey
mother–one another
mouth–north and south
neck–bushel and peck
night–flying kite
nose–I suppose
paper or newspaper–linen draper
pillow–weeping willow
pipe–cherry ripe
plate–Harry Tate
pocket–sky rocket
policeman (cop)–John Hop

room—shovel and broom
shirt—Dickey dirt
sick—Pat and Mick or Uncle Dick
sister—skin and blister
sleep or asleep—Bopeep
socks—almond rocks
stairs—apples and pears
steal (pinch)—half inch
street—fields of wheat
table—Cain and Abel
talk—bowl of chalk
tea—bug and flea or sweet pea
tobacco—nosey-me-knacker
trousers—round me houses or round the houses
umbrella—Isabella
walk—whisper and talk
water—fisherman's daughter
wife—trouble and strife

Mince pie put on my Dickey dirt and new daisy roots and went down the apples and pears to see the cows and kisses.

Activities With Rhyming Slang

1. Use the rhyming slang phrases in writing sentences and short stories.
2. Make up your own rhyming slang phrases.
3. Collect rhyming phrases such as hot shot, culture vulture, and sure cure.

SLANG WORDS AND PHRASES

We no longer need to consult a dictionary for the meanings of *hubbub, clumsy, bogus,* or *beat it,* used by Shakespeare, or for *bones* (dice) used by Chaucer. These words were considered slang in their times. Today's slang terms often have multiple meanings and are more difficult to define precisely. To provide a challenging activity, duplicate this list *without* definitions and ask the children to supply their own meanings.

all right—expression of emphatic agreement; exclamation of approval
bag—a special interest or enthusiasm
blew it—failed or missed an opportunity
blow your mind—to be overwhelmed or deeply impressed
bombed out (bombed)—failed or did very poorly
bummer—a bad experience or situation
cool—pleasing; in good taste
cool it—calm down
cop out—to renege on a plan or a promise

cracked up—had a fit of laughter
dig—to understand or enjoy; to notice or look at someone
downer—a depressing experience or situation
drag—boring; tedious person, thing, or event
dynamite—fantastic; terrific
far out—expression of approval; out of the ordinary
flake—unpredictable, irresponsible person
fox—attractive female
freak—person who likes a certain thing to an extreme
freak out—become irrational; shock others by unconventional behavior
funk, in a—in a depressed mood
funky—pleasing in an out-of-the-ordinary way
groovy—very good
hairy—frightening; difficult; exciting
hang in there—refuse to give in
hang tough—refuse to give in
heavy—deep; meaningful; profound
hung up—obsessed with; devoted to
hype—trick, deceive; promote
hyped up—overly excited
jive—tease; deceive
kicky—in fashion; exciting
laid back—easygoing; low-keyed
kinky—bizarre; peculiar
nerd, nurd—a person not in the know; a "square"
no sweat—no problem; easily
out of sight—great; wonderful
out of it—not involved with the present situation; not in the know; "square"
pad—place where a person lives
plastic—artificial
psyched out—fooled, misled; lost nerve or control due to fear or anxiety
psyched up—mentally prepared
put down—humiliating act or remark
really—a statement of agreement
right on—exclamation of approval
rip off—to steal; to defraud
solid—great; wonderful
spaced—not in touch with reality
tee'd off—angry
turkey—inferior, ineffective, incompetent person or thing
turn-on—interesting or exciting person or thing
unreal—unbelievably wonderful

up front—honest; open
uptight—anxious; rigid
wimp—a meek, uninteresting person
wiped out—tired; exhausted

Activities With Slang Words and Phrases

1. Make "Slang Synonym Serpents."

2. Define slang words and phrases using other slang in your definitions.
3. Many of the slang words and phrases can be used to name or describe people, situations, or feelings. Categorize the words into these groups.

PEOPLE	SITUATIONS	FEELINGS
flake	bummer	in a funk
cool	cool	

4. Expand the list of slang words and phrases by adding other forms of the terms. Indicate what part of speech they are and write sentences to show how they are used.

rip off (noun)	The rock concert was a real rip off.
rip off (verb)	Jeff was ripped off at the used car lot.

HELLO AND GOODBYE

Language	Hello or Good Day	Goodbye
Chinese ("Mandarin" dialect)	dzǎu	dzàijyàn
Danish	hallo	farvel
French	bon jour	au revoir
German	guten tag	auf Wiedersehen
Hawaiian	aloha	aloha
Hebrew	shalom	shalom
Italian	buon giorno	addio
Farsi (Iran)	salaam سلام	khoda hafez خدا حافظ
Polish	hallo	żegnam
Portuguese	alô	adeus
Russian	Здравствуйте	до свидания
pronunciation	ZDRAHST-vooy-tyeh	daw svee-DA-nee-ya
Swahili	neno la kusalimu rafiki au mtani	kwa heri
Tagalog (Philippines)	kumusta	paalám
Spanish	holá	adiós
Swedish	god dag	adjö
Thai	sa wat dee ka	la kone na ka

PART **2**

SIGNS, SYMBOLS, TELESCOPES, & T-SQUARES

six

SIGNS & SYMBOLS

MATH SIGNS AND SYMBOLS

+	addition sign, plus, positive
−	subtraction sign, minus, negative
±	plus or minus
X	multiplication sign, multiplied by, times
÷	division sign, divided by
=	equals, is equal to
≠	is not equal to
<	less than
>	greater than
≪	much less than
≫	much greater than
$	dollar sign
¢	cent(s)
£	pound sign used for monetary units (such as the Israeli and British pound)
∷	as, equals
∴	therefore
∵	since, because
△	triangle
□	square
▭	rectangle
∟	right angle
∠	angle
r	radius
d	diameter
π	Pi, the number 3.1416
≅	congruent, is congruent to
→	ray
⊥	perpendicular, is perpendicular to
∥	parallel, is parallel to
@	at
#	number or pound
%	percent
°	degree(s)
∞	infinity
:	is to, the ratio of
√	square root
{ }	indicates a set
φ	empty set

HOBO SIGNS

Hobo signs are usually drawn with chalk on fences, sidewalks, trees, or poles to tell the next hobo passing by what to expect in a town or place.

KIND LADY LIVES HERE

VICIOUS DOG HERE

A GENTLEMAN LIVES HERE

THESE PEOPLE ARE RICH

WATCH OUT FOR THIEVES

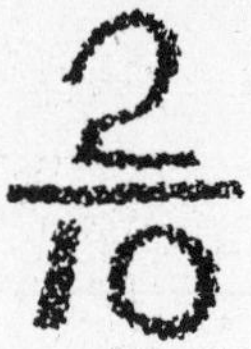

YOU CAN SLEEP IN HAYLOFT

OR

TELL A SAD STORY

WOMAN LIVES HERE

YOU CAN GET FOOD HERE BY WORKING

OR

DOCTOR HERE, WON'T CHARGE

FREE TELEPHONE

JAIL

IF SICK, WILL CARE FOR YOU

KEEP QUIET

HOLD YOUR TONGUE

BARKING DOG HERE

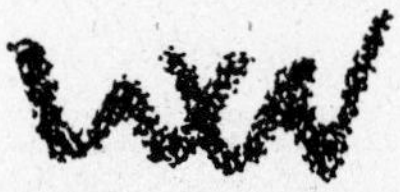

BEWARE OF FOUR DOGS

YOU CAN CAMP HERE

DRINKING WATER, SAFE CAMP

DANGEROUS DRINKING WATER

O.K., ALL RIGHT

MAN WITH A GUN LIVES HERE

OPEN EYE, POLICE ARE LOOKING FOR HOBOES

CLOSED EYE, POLICE NOT LOOKING FOR HOBOES

NOTHING TO BE GAINED HERE

GOOD PLACE FOR A HANDOUT

TROLLEY STOP

GOOD PLACE TO CATCH A TRAIN

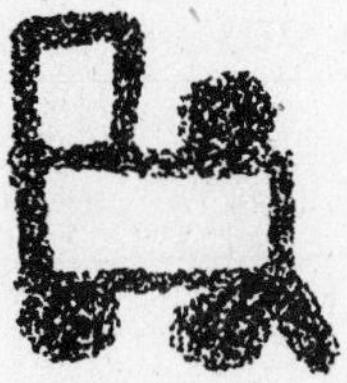

THIS IS NOT A SAFE PLACE

DANGER

NO USE GOING THIS DIRECTION

THIS WAY

HIT THE ROAD! QUICK! GO!

OR

HALT

DANGEROUS NEIGHBORHOOD

DISHONEST PERSON LIVES HERE

COWARDS, WILL GIVE, TO GET RID OF YOU

CRIME COMMITTED, NOT SAFE FOR STRANGERS

JUDGE LIVES HERE

COURTHOUSE; PRECINCT STATION

OFFICER OF LAW LIVES HERE

Name

HOBO SIGNS

1. Draw a hobo sign on each object pictured below.
2. Under each picture write the meaning of the signs you've drawn.
3. On the back of this page, or on another sheet of paper, write a story telling what happened to cause a hobo to leave these signs.

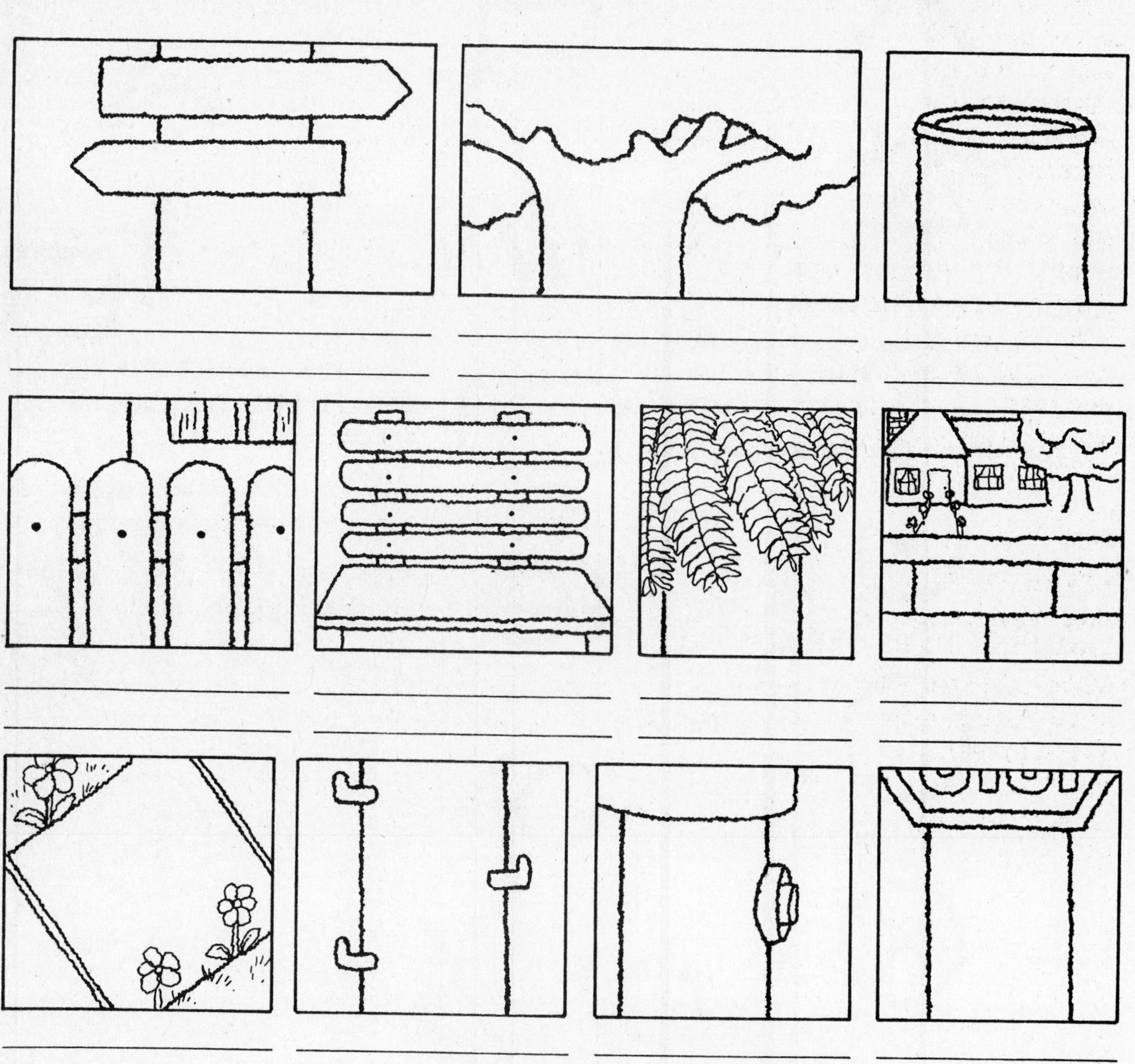

X MARKS THE SPOT–X'S AND O'S

The X's and O's list can add to children's understanding that information can be communicated symbolically in many ways, including the use of letters. Children may wish to illustrate some of these symbolic meanings and collect examples of the use of X, O, and other letters from magazines, newspapers, and product packages and wrappings.

X's

multiplication sign; times
by, as in 4′ x 4′
a tic tac toe sign
railroad crossing
marks a spot on a map
Roman numeral ten
as in brand X
closed lane
a vote
a way to sign your name if you don't know how to write
axis, used in mathematics
cross out
a kiss in a letter or note
an unknown amount

O's

oxygen
some highway markers
zero
a hug in a letter or note
some cities on maps
a tic tac toe sign
ceiling outlet on a blueprint
empty set (ϕ)

COMIC STRIP SYMBOLS

Many ideas in comic strips are communicated without the use of words. Following are some common comic strip symbols and their usual meanings.

COMIC STRIP WORDS

AAAAGH
AAA-CHOO
AARGH
AH-HAAA
ARRGGG
BANG
BLAM
BOM
BONG
BONK
BOO
BZZ-ZT
CRACK
EEEYAAAA
GLOM
HAH
HA-HA-HA-HA-HA
HISS
KER-PLOP
KLINK
KWAM
KWOMP
OOOO-OH
PHZZZ
POOF
POW
SNIP
SPLAM
THUD
UGH
UNGAAA
UNGARRR
WHAM
WHAP
WHOMP
WHOOSH
WHUMP
WOK
YEOWW
YYYYIIII
ZAK
ZAP

COMIC STRIP FACIAL EXPRESSIONS

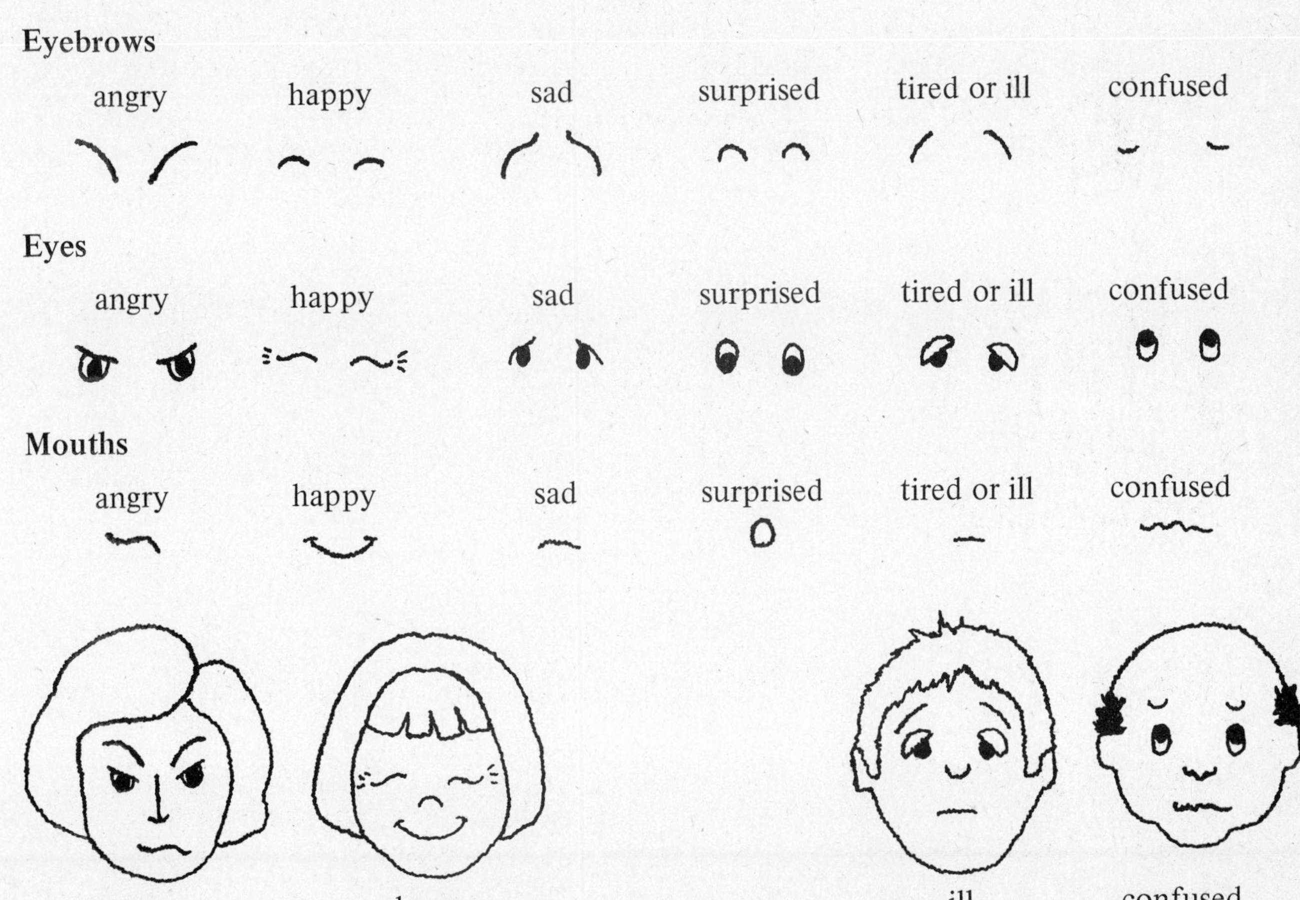

Comic Strip Activities

1. Draw a strip using only symbols, facial expressions, and comic strip words to communicate the story.
2. Select several comic strip words. Describe or illustrate situations in which they would be used.
3. Cut out examples from real comic strips to match any of the symbols, facial expressions, or comic strip words on the lists.
4. Cut out photographs of people or animals from newspapers and magazines. Label them with appropriate comic strip symbols or words.
5. Write an autobiography or biography of a cartoon character.
6. Keep a journal to summarize a strip day-by-day.

CHEMICAL SYMBOLS

"Dr. Strangebrain locked the door to his lab and stirred up the secret compound of two parts Uranium, one part Antimony, and three parts Lithium. He recorded the compound in his log:

"2U + 1Sb + 3Li."

A smattering of chemical names and symbols can add authentic-sounding details to children's stories of mad scientists and crazy chemists.

Actinium–Ac
Aluminum–Al
Americium–Am
Antimony–Sb
Argon–Ar
Arsenic–As
Astatine–At
Barium–Ba
Berkelium–Bk
Beryllium–Be
Bismuth–Bi
Boron–B
Bromine–Br
Cadmium–Cd
Calcium–Ca
Californium–Cf
Carbon–C
Cerium–Ce
Cesium–Cs
Chlorine–Cl
Chromium–Cr
Cobalt–Co
Copper–Cu
Curium–Cm
Dysprosium–Dy
Einsteinium–Es
Erbium–Er
Europium–Eu
Fermium–Fm
Fluorine–F
Francium–Fr
Gadolinium–Gd
Gallium–Ga
Germanium–Ge
Gold–Au
Hafnium–Hf
Helium–He
Holmium–Ho
Hydrogen–H
Indium–In
Iodine–I
Iridium–In
Iron–Fe
Krypton–Kr
Lanthanum–La
Lawrencium–Lr
Lead–Pb
Lithium–Li
Lutetium–Lu
Magnesium–Mg
Manganese–Mn
Mendelevium–Md
Mercury–Hg
Molybdenum–Mo
Neodymium–Nd
Neon–Ne
Neptunium–Np
Nickel–Ni
Niobium
(Columbium) Nb
Nitrogen–N
Nobelium–No
Osmium–Os
Oxygen–O
Palladium–Pd
Phosphorus–P
Platinum–Pt
Plutonium–Pu
Polonium–Po
Potassium–K
Praseodymium–Pr
Promethium–Pm
Protactinium–Pa
Radium–Ra
Radon–Rn
Rhenium–Re
Rhodium–Rh
Rubidium–Rb
Ruthenium–Ru
Samarium–Sm
Scandium–Sc
Selenium–Se
Silicon–Si
Silver–Ag
Sodium–Na
Strontium–Sr
Sulfur–S
Tantalum–Ta
Technetium–Tc
Tellurium–Te
Terbium–Tb
Thallium–Tl
Thorium–Th
Thulium–Tm
Tin–Sn
Titanium–Ti
Tungsten (Wolfram)–W
Uranium–U
Vanadium–V
Xenon–Xe
Ytterbium–Yb
Yttrium–Y
Zinc–Zn
Zirconium–Zr

INTERNATIONAL MORSE CODE

Samuel Morse telegraphed this message, "What hath God wrought." Children can transmit their own messages, spelling words, and math problems by tapping with a pencil or by using a telegraph (have your mechanical wizard make one).

A .–
B –...
C –.–.
D –..
E .
F ..–.
G ––.
H ....
I ..
J .–––
K –.–
L .–..
M ––
N –.
O –––
P .––.
Q ––.–
R .–.
S ...
T –
U ..–
V ...–
W .––
X –..–
Y –.––
Z ––..
1 .––––
2 ..–––
3 ...––
4 ....–
5 .....
6 –....
7 ––...
8 –––..
9 ––––.
0 –––––
Period .–.–.–
Comma ––..––
Question Mark ..––..
Colon –––...
Semicolon –.–.–.
Quotation marks .–..–.

Some brief forms often used in communications:

AR (end of message) .–.–.
EEEEEEE (error) ....
A (affirmative-yes) .–
N (negative-no) –.
R (message received and understood) .–.
SOS (distress signal) ...–––...

TIME OUT—IMPORTANT FOOTBALL AND BASKETBALL SIGNALS

Football

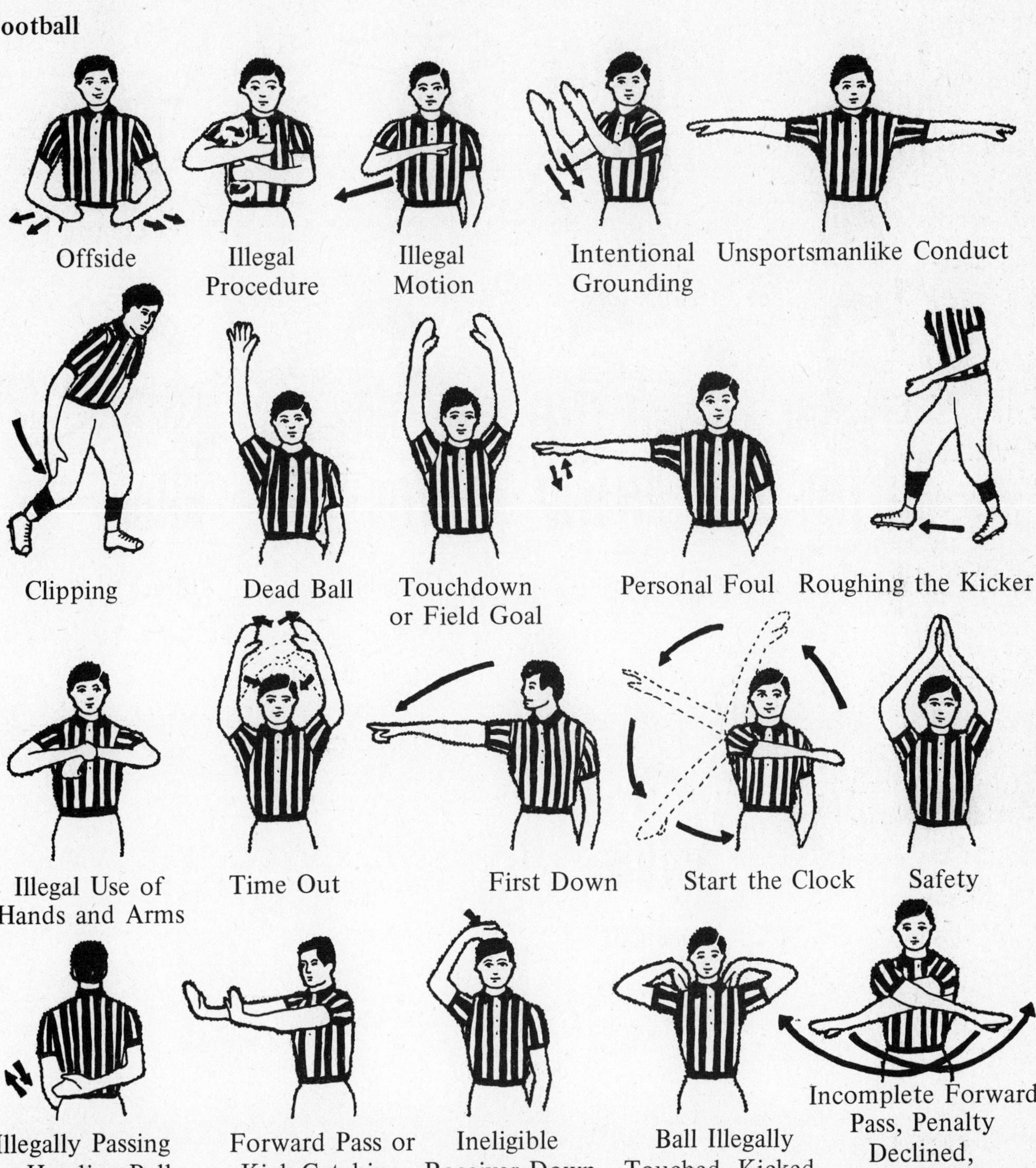

Basketball

Personal Foul

Illegal Use of Hands

Pushing

Player Control Foul

Holding

Technical Foul

Traveling

Illegal Dribble

Cancel Score

Time Out

HAND ALPHABET

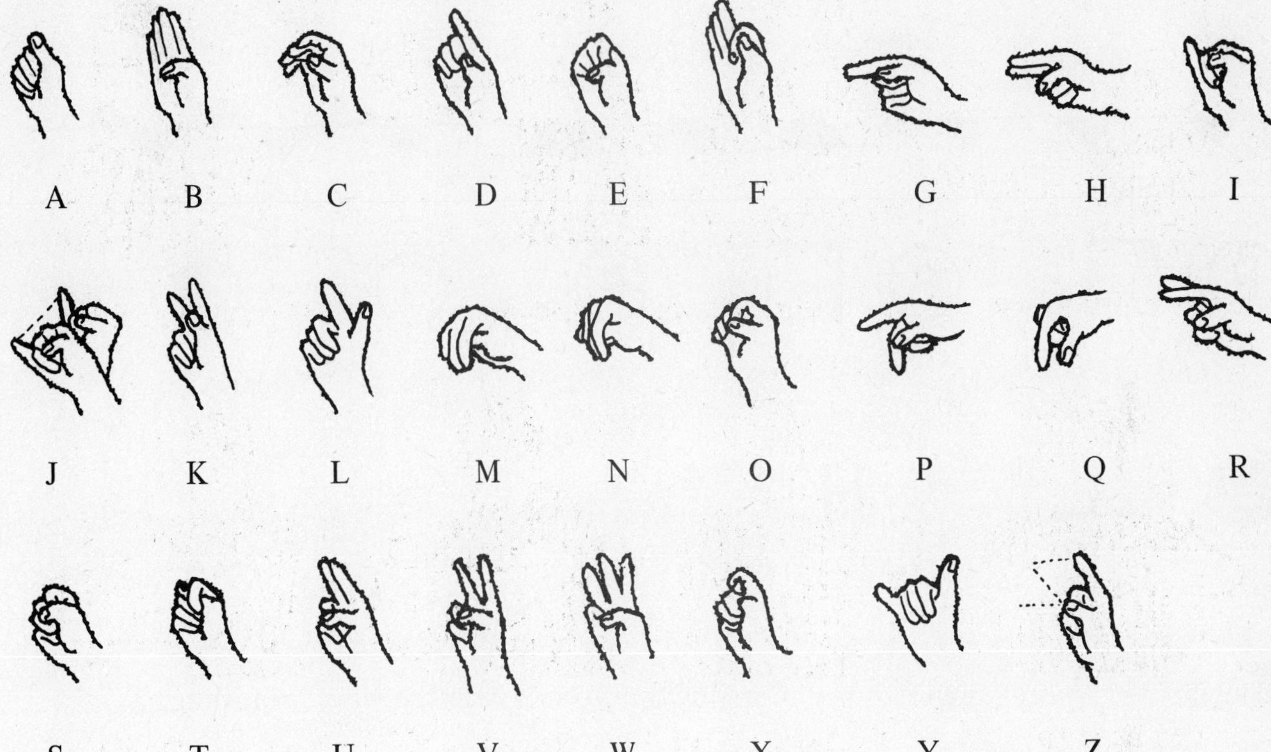

WEATHER SYMBOLS

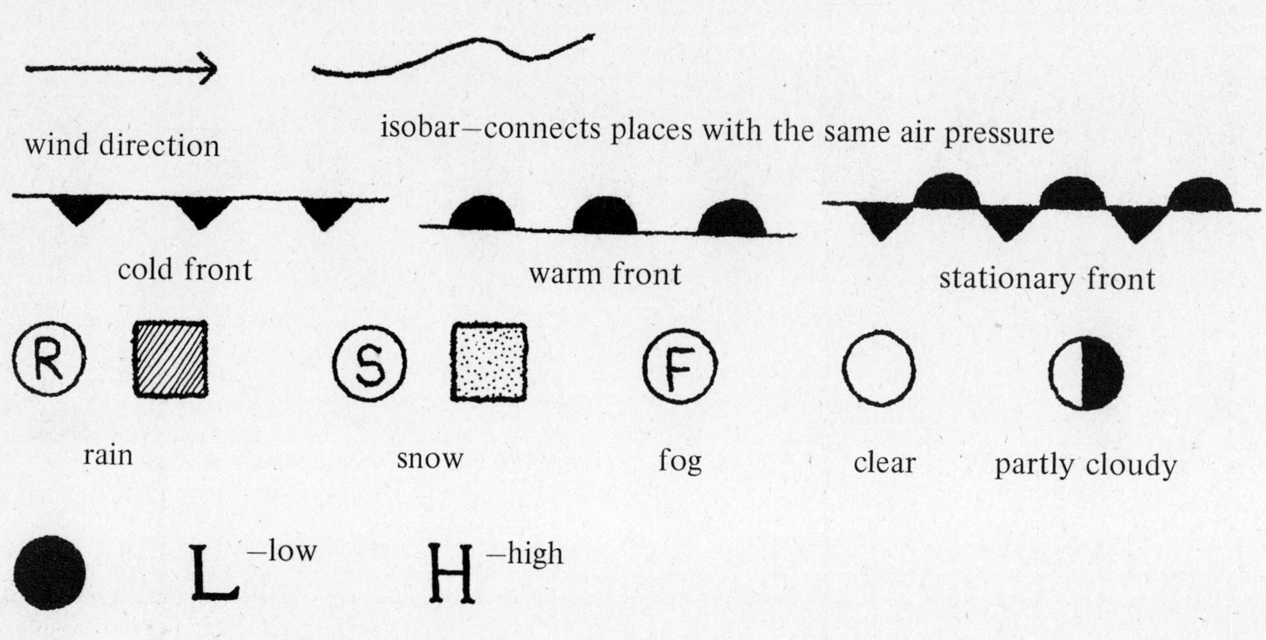

Wind and cloud cover—tail points in the direction from which the wind is blowing.

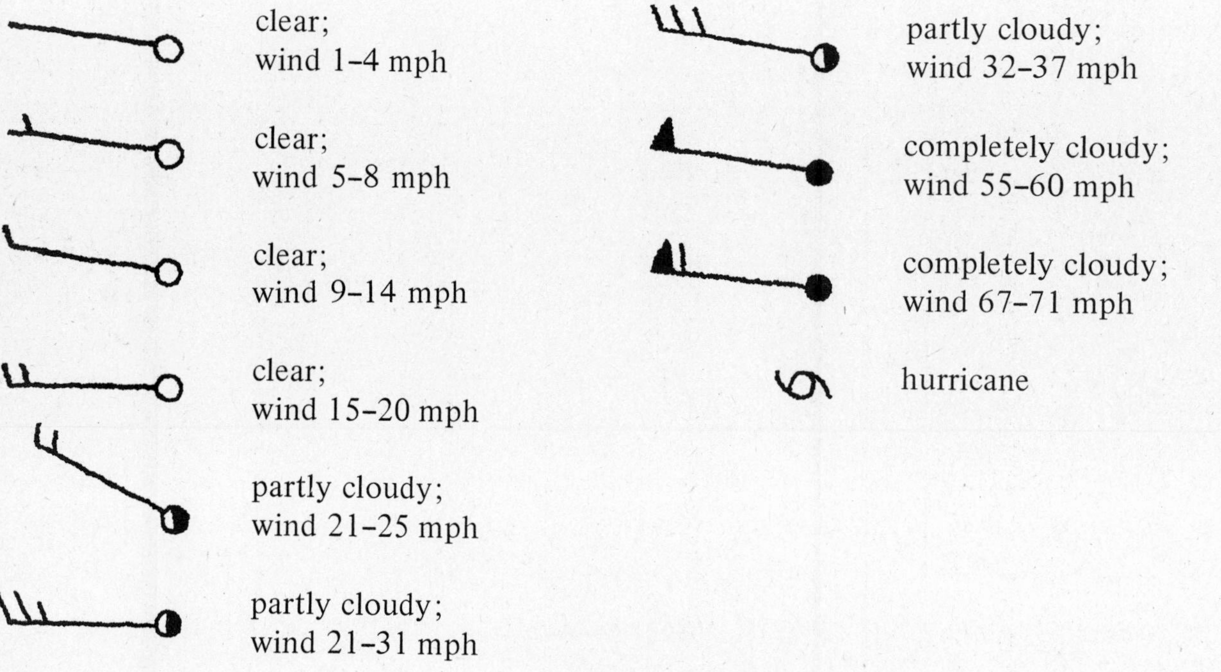

Name ______________________________

WHAT'S THE WEATHER?

Directions: Read the weather report. Mark the map with weather symbols that go with the report. Draw three more weather symbols on the map and complete the weatherman's report for the symbols you've added.

A cold front is moving across Oregon bringing snow. Over Texas it is partly cloudy with winds of 23 mph blowing from the north. Southern California continues to be rainy. ______________________________

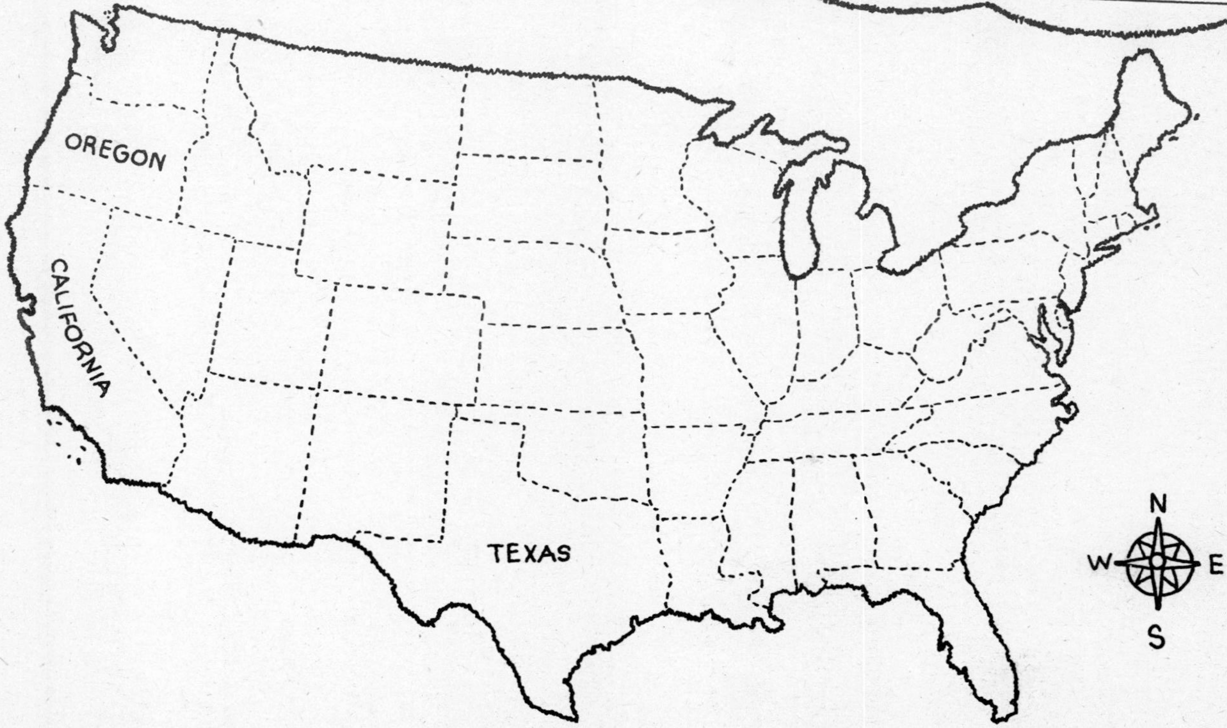

____

____

OREGON

CALIFORNIA

TEXAS

N

W

E

S

MAP SYMBOLS

state capitals

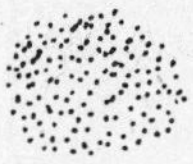

campground

mountain peak

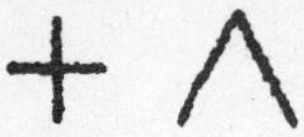

skiing

swamp

public parks, picnic areas

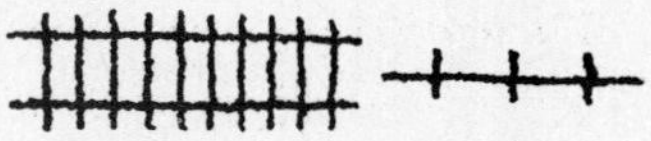

lake

dry lake

bridge

city

tunnel

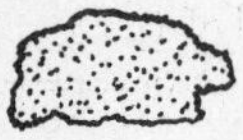

desert

church

school

hospital

railroad

airport

waterfall

canal

river

point of interest

forest

Name

MAPMAKERS

Draw symbols on the map and make up a name for each. In the Map Index list each place name and the letter and number that shows its location.

	A	B	C	D	E	F	G	H
1								
2								
3								
4								
5								
6						Tall Pines Campground		
7								

MAP INDEX

Tall Pines Campground F6

RED LIGHT/GREEN LIGHT—SYMBOLIC USES OF COLOR

Colors are often used to communicate meaning symbolically, without words. Here are some examples for red and green.

Red lights and their usual meanings:

Automobile brake lights—car is stopping or slowing down

Automobile dashboard—warning (brake is set, gas or oil is needed)

Doors or halls—exit here

Electrical appliances—appliance is on or hot

Railroads—stop

Traffic lights—stop

TV Studios—don't come in now (filming is in progress)

Vending machines—empty or out of a given item

Other uses of red:

Red flag at the beach—heavy, dangerous surf

Red letters or markings—flammable materials; fire-fighting equipment

Red ribbon—second place in a contest

Idioms based on red:

blood-red—having the deep-red color of blood

in the red—in debt

paint the town red—have an exciting time

red carpet treatment—extra-special treatment

red letter day—memorable or happy day

red tape—complicated procedure

sees red—is angry

Green lights and their usual meanings:

Railroads—track is clear

Traffic light—go

Other uses of green:

Green flag at the beach—average surf

Green flag in racing—start

Green power—ecology

Green letters or markings—safety

Idioms based on green:

greenbacks—paper currency

greenhorn—inexperienced person

green with envy or jealousy

green thumb—a talent for growing plants

green around the gills—sick

Activities For Red Light/Green Light

1. Make a priority list of the red lights and other red things in order from what is most important to what is least important for survival. Do the same for green.
2. Illustrate each of the idioms to show their literal meanings.
3. Add other colors and some of their symbolic meanings to the list.

seven

TELESCOPES & T-SQUARES

PLANET TABLE

The Planet Table can be the basis for many math activities. Older children can convert years to days, days to hours, hours to seconds, miles to kilometers, compute sums for each column, and make up problems for other children to solve. You may wish to round off some of the numbers to make them easier for children to work with.

	Average Distance From Sun (Miles)	Diameter (Miles)	Period of Revolution	Period of Rotation	Known Moons	Probable Temperature in °F	To Find Your Weight, Multiply Your Weight By:
Mercury	35,960,000	3,100	88 days	57 days	0	+600	0.27
Venus	67,200,000	7,700	225 days	247 days	0	+100	0.85
Earth	92,900,000	7,918	365¼ days	23 hrs 56 mins	1	+50	1.00
Mars	141,500,000	4,200	687 days	24 hrs 37 mins	2	+0	0.38
Jupiter	483,400,000	89,000	11.86 years	9 hrs 55 mins	13	-150	2.64
Saturn	886,200,000	71,500	29.5 years	10 hrs 14 mins	10	-250	1.17
Uranus	1,783,000,000	30,000	84 years	10 hrs 45 mins	5	-350	0.92
Neptune	2,790,000,000	27,700	164.75 years	15 hrs 45 mins	2	-400	1.12
Pluto	3,670,000,000	3,664	248.5 years	6.4 days	0	?	?

Planet Table Activities

1. Calculate what your weight would be on each planet.
2. Rewrite any or all of the columns in number words rather than numerals.

3. Compute the differences between any two planets for each of the features shown on the table. Write statements to show your findings.

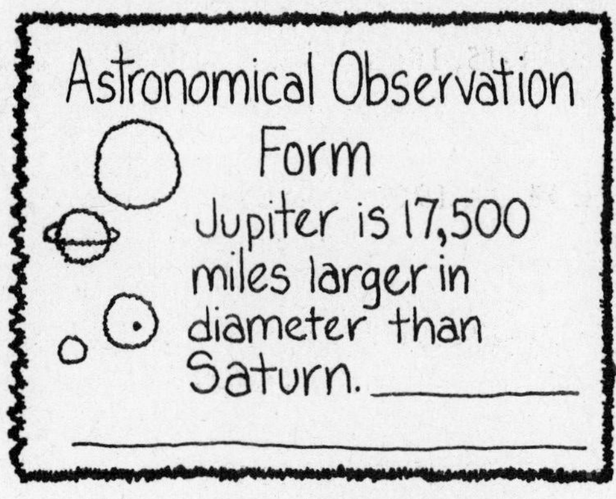

4. Design a travel brochure or poster for one of the planets. Use your imagination. It's okay to be unscientific.

FLY ME TO THE MOON—NOTABLE U.S. SPACE MISSIONS

Date	Mission	Crew	Duration (Hr:Min:Sec)	
May 5, 1961	Mercury-Redstone 3	Shepard	00:15:22	First American in space; a suborbital flight
Feb. 20, 1962	Mercury-Atlas 6	Glenn	04:55:23	First American in orbit; a three-orbit flight
June 3–7, 1965	Gemini-Titan IV	McDivitt, White	97:56:11	White becomes the first American to walk in space (20 minutes)
March 16, 1966	Gemini-Titan VIII	Armstrong, Scott	10:41:26	First docking of one space vehicle with another
June 3–6, 1966	Gemini-Titan IX-A	Stafford, Cernan	72:21:00	Cernan carried out 2 hours 7 minutes extravehicular activity
Sept. 12–15, 1966	Gemini-Titan XI	Conrad, Gordon	71:17:08	Gemini set a record altitude of 739.2 miles

Nov. 11–15, 1966	Gemini-Titan XII	Lovell, Aldrin	94:34:31	Final Gemini flight; Aldrin set a record total of 5 hours 30 minutes of extravehicular activity
Oct. 11–22, 1968	Apollo-Saturn 7	Schirra, Eisele, Cunningham	260:09:03	First manned flight of Apollo spacecraft
Dec. 21–27, 1968	Apollo-Saturn 8	Borman, Lovell, Anders	147:00:42	First flight to the moon; views of lunar surface televised to earth
March 3–13, 1969	Apollo-Saturn 9	McDivitt, Scott, Schweickart	241:00:54	First manned flight of lunar module
July 16–24, 1969	Apollo-Saturn 11	Armstrong, Collins, Aldrin	195:18:35	First lunar landing (in the Sea of Tranquility); lunar stay time 21:36:21; took lunar surface samples of 48.5 pounds
July 26–Aug. 7, 1971	Apollo-Saturn 15	Scott, Worden, Irwin	295:11:53	Fourth lunar landing; first use of lunar roving vehicle
Dec. 7–19, 1972	Apollo-Saturn 17	Cernan, Evans, Schmitt	301:51:59	Last Apollo flight to moon
May 25–June 22, 1973	Skylab 2	Conrad, Kerwin, Weitz	672:49:49 (28 days)	First U.S. manned orbiting space station mission
Nov. 16, 1973–Feb. 8, 1974	Skylab 4	Carr, Gibson, Pogue	2017:16:30 (84 days)	Final Skylab manned visit; longest flight of men in space; made observations of Comet Kohoutek; set record for space walk–7 hours, 1 minute
July 17, 1975 (Rendezvous and Docking)	Apollo-Soyuz Test Project	U.S.: Stafford, Brand, Slayton Russia: Leonov, Kubasov		First docking between U.S. and Russian spacecraft; cosmonauts and astronauts visited each other's spacecraft

The next major space mission will be the Space Shuttle, planned for 1980.

SOURCE: NASA

A Dozen Debriefing Questions to be used with Fly Me to the Moon, p. 104 and 105.

1. Who was the first American to walk in space?

___

2. Which was the first flight to the moon?

___

3. What was the site of the first lunar landing?

___

4. When did the first manned orbiting space station mission begin?

___

5. During which mission did the first manned flight of the lunar module occur?

___

6. Who were the astronauts who set a Gemini altitude record?

___

7. Of the notable space missions listed, which was the longest Gemini flight? How much longer was it than the shortest Gemini flight?

___

8. How much time did Scott spend in space according to the list?

___

9. What notable space event occurred on July 17, 1975?

___

10. What piece of equipment was used for the first time on the Apollo-Saturn 15 mission?

___

11. What were the two notable missions Armstrong was on?

___

12. Including the walks in space, what was the total time of extravehicular activity reported?

___

SPACE TALK—SPACE TERMS USED IN AIR-TO-GROUND COMMUNICATION

Booster, bugs, foxtrot, footprints, and the Brooklyn Clothesline will become familiar words as children develop play and radio dialogues and reenactments of extraterrestrial travel based on the following Space Talk vocabulary. Children will want to make props, such as instrument panels and spacecraft models, incorporating items from the list.

ABORT—to cut short a mission or launch due to problems

ALL BALLS—flight crew slang for all zeroes

ALPHA—alphabet designation for the letter A

AMBIENT—the environmental condition, such as temperature, air pressure

APOGEE—the highest point in an orbit around earth

AUDIO SYSTEM—voice portion of communications system

BACKUP—item or system kept on hand to replace one that fails; astronaut or crew used to replace the prime crew in the event of illness

BARBER POLES—small gauges on control panels that are striped diagonally in black and white

BECO—booster engine cut-off

BLACKOUT—a fadeout of radio communication between a spacecraft and the ground during reentry

BLOCKHOUSE—Launch Control Center at Pad 39, Cape Kennedy

BOOSTER—launch vehicle

BRAVO—alphabet designation for the letter B

BREAKING UP—a garbling of voice transmission

BROOKLYN CLOTHESLINE—a loop of rope on pulleys used to transport film during extravehicular activities (EVAs)

BUG—an unidentified problem

BURN—the firing of engines

BUTTON UP—to completely close or seal any unit or vehicle such as the spacecraft

CHARLIE—alphabet designation for the letter C

CSM—COMMAND AND SERVICE MODULE—three-man spacecraft used in Apollo; same type of vehicle used to transport crews and equipment to and from Skylab

COMMAND MODULE—the crew portion of the CSM (see above definition)

COPY—synonym for read (understand, as during a voice transmission)

COUNTDOWN—step-by-step preparation for launch

DAMPING—restraining; slowing down or stopping

DEBRIEFING—questioning of crewmen after a mission to obtain useful information

DEBUG—remove problems or malfunctions from a system

DELTA—alphabet designation for the letter D

DEORBIT—coming out of an earth orbit into splashdown trajectory

DOWN IN THE MUD—slang for very low volume in radio reception

DOWNTIME—time during which a system is not in condition or functioning

DRAG—resistance of the air to a body in motion

ECHO—alphabet designation for the letter E

EGRESS—to exit the spacecraft

EVA—extravehicular activity

FIVE BY FIVE—a term denoting radio reception is loud and clear

FOOTPRINT—the area of possible landing points for a vehicle at reentry

FOXTROT—alphabet designation for the letter F

GLITCH—a problem of any nature, especially during countdown

GOLF—alphabet designation for the letter G

HANDOVER—to pass spacecraft communication from one tracking station to another

HOLD—a delay in the launch countdown

HOTEL—alphabet designation for the letter H

INDIA—alphabet designation for the letter I

INGRESS—to enter the spacecraft

JETTISON—to discard into space

JULIET—alphabet designation for the letter J

KILO—alphabet designation for the letter K

LAUNCH VEHICLE—the booster as opposed to the spacecraft

LAUNCH WINDOW—the limited frame of time during which launch can be accomplished

LIMA—alphabet designation for the letter L

MIKE—alphabet designation for the letter M

MURPHY'S LAW—a so-called "scientific" law that states "What can go wrong will go wrong"

NO GO—indicates something is functioning improperly; not ready to proceed

NO JOY—slang meaning an expected event has not happened or a looked-for object has not been located

NOVEMBER—alphabet designation for the letter N

OPEN ENDED MISSION—a flight of no specific duration; continues as long as equipment functions properly

OSCAR—alphabet designation for the letter O

PAPA—alphabet designation for the letter P

PASS—the passage of a spacecraft over a tracking station or target area

PIGTAIL—a short, coiled wire or bundle of wires

POLL THE ROOM—take a consensus of flight controllers before making a go or no go decision

POO—Program Zero-Zero—clearing the spacecraft computer

POT—potable, drinkable

PUSH-TO-TALK—microphone switch which is pressed when a crewman wishes to transmit his voice

Q-BALL—device in nose cone of launch escape system which provides information

QUEBEC—alphabet designation for the letter Q

READ—understand, as during a voice transmission

REAL TIME—indicates the reporting of events at the nearly instantaneous time they occur

REV—revolution

ROGER—okay; will do

ROMEO—alphabet designation for the letter R

R & R—rest and recreation

SCRUB—to cancel or postpone a flight

SHOT—slang for launch or flight

SIERRA—alphabet designation for the letter S

SKIN TRACKING—tracking by radar bounced off the outside of the vehicle

SOM—start of message

SPLASHDOWN—impact of the spacecraft in the ocean during landing

TANGO—alphabet designation for the letter T

THRUST—push; force developed by a rocket engine

TOK—thrust O.K.

UNIFORM—alphabet designation for the letter U

VICTOR—alphabet designation for the letter V

WARMER—flight control slang for "better"

WHISKEY—alphabet designation for the letter W

WILCO—pilot slang for "will comply"

YANKEE—alphabet designation for the letter Y

ZIPS—all zeroes

ZULU—alphabet designation for the letter Z

MEASUREMENT ABBREVIATIONS

Metric Abbreviations

nanometer–nm
millimeter–mm
centimeter–cm
decimeter–dm
meter–m
dekameter–dam
hectometer–hm
kilometer–km

milliliter–ml
centiliter–cl
deciliter–dl
liter–l
dekaliter–dal
hectoliter–hl
kiloliter–kl

milligram–mg
centigram–cg
decigram–dg
gram–g
dekagram–dag
hectogram–hg
kilogram–kg
metric ton–t

square millimeter–mm^2
square centimeter–cm^2
square meter–m^2
are–a
hectare–ha
square kilometer–km^2

cubic millimeter–mm^3
cubic centimeter–cm^3
cubic decimeter–dm^3
cubic meter–m^3

Other Measurement Abbreviations

inch–in, ″
foot–ft, ′
yard–yd
rod–rd
furlong–fur
mile–mi

gill–gi
pint–pt
quart–qt
gallon–gal

peck–pk
bushel–bu

chain–ch

cup–c
teaspoon–t, tsp
tablespoon–T, tbsp

grain–gr
pennyweight–dwt
ounce troy–oz t
pound troy–lb t

dram–dr
ounce–oz
pound–lb, #
hundredweight–cwt
ton–t

second–sec, ″
minute–min, ′
hour–hr
day–da
week–wk
month–mo
year–yr

barrel–bbl
cord–cd
fathom–fm

WEIGHTS AND MEASURES

Metric Weights and Measures

Length

10 millimeters	= 1 centimeter	
10 centimeters	= 1 decimeter	= 100 mm
10 decimeters	= 1 meter	= 1000 mm
10 meters	= 1 dekameter	
10 dekameters	= 1 hectometer	= 100 m
10 hectometers	= 1 kilometer	= 1000 m

Liquid

10 milliliters	= 1 centiliter	
10 centiliters	= 1 deciliter	= 100 ml
10 deciliters	= 1 liter	= 1000 ml
10 liters	= 1 dekaliter	
10 dekaliters	= 1 hectoliter	= 100 liters
10 hectoliters	= 1 kiloliter	= 1000 liters

Liquid

8 drams	= 1 ounce	
4 gills	= 1 pint	= 16 ounces
2 pints	= 1 quart	= 8 gills
4 quarts	= 1 gallon	= 8 pints = 32 gills
31½ gallons	= 1 barrel	= 126 quarts
2 barrels	= 1 hogshead	= 63 gallons
		= 252 quarts

Dry

2 pints	= 1 quart	
8 quarts	= 1 peck	= 16 pints
4 pecks	= 1 bushel	= 32 quarts
		= 64 pints
105 quarts	= 1 barrel	

Volume

1,728 cubic inches	= 1 cubic foot
27 cubic feet	= 1 cubic yard
144 cubic inches	= 1 board foot
128 cubic feet	= 1 cord

Angular and Circular Measure

60 seconds	= 1 minute
60 minutes	= 1 degree
90 degrees	= 1 quadrant
180 degrees	= 1 straight angle
360 degrees	= 1 circle = 4 quadrants

Length

12 inches	= 1 foot	
3 feet	= 1 yard	
5½ yards	= 1 rod, pole, or perch (16½ ft)	
40 rods	= 1 furlong	= 220 yards
		= 660 feet
8 furlongs	= 1 statute mile	= 1,760 yards
		= 5,280 ft.
3 miles	= 1 league	= 5,280 yds.
		= 15,840 ft.

Area

144 square inches	= 1 square foot
9 square feet	= 1 square yard
	= 9 sq. ft. = 1,296 sq. in.
30¼ square rods	= 1 sq. rod
	= 272¼ sq. ft.
960 square rods	= 1 acre
	= 4,840 sq. yds.
	= 43,560 sq. ft.
1 square mile	= 640 acres
6 miles square	= 1 township
	= 36 sections
	= 36 square miles

Weight—Avoirdupois

27 11/32 grains	= 1 dram	
16 drams	= 1 ounce	= 437.5 grains
16 ounces	= 1 pound	= 256 drams
		= 7,000 grains
100 pounds	= 1 hundredweight	
20 hundredweights	= 1 ton	= 2,000 pounds
20 long hundredweights	= 1 long ton	
	= 2,240 pounds	

Weight—Troy

24 grains	= 1 pennyweight	
20 pennyweights	= 1 ounce troy	= 480 grains
12 ounces troy	= 1 pound troy	
	= 240 pennyweights	
	= 5,760 grains	

Volume

1000 cubic millimeters	= 1 cubic centimeter
1000 cubic centimeters	= 1 cubic decimeter
	= 1,000,000 mm^3
1000 cubic decimeters	= 1 cubic meter
	= 1 stere
	= 1,000,000 cm^3
	= 1,000,000,000 mm^3

Area

100 square millimeters	= 1 square centimeter
100 square centimeters	= 1 square decimeter
100 square decimeters	= 1 square meter
	= 10,000 cm^2
	= 1,000,000 mm^2
100 square meters	= 1 are
10 ares	= 1 hectare
	= 10,000 m^2
100 hectares	= 1 square kilometer
	= 1,000,000 m^2

Weight

10 milligrams	= 1 centigram	
10 centigrams	= 1 decigram	= 100 mg
10 decigrams	= 1 gram	= 1,000 mg
10 grams	= 1 dekagram	
10 dekagrams	= 1 hectogram	= 100 grams
10 hectograms	= 1 kilogram	= 1,000 grams
100 kilograms	= 1 quintal	
10 quintals	= 1 metric ton	
	= 1,000 kilograms	

GEOMETRIC FORMULAS

To find the circumference of a

CIRCLE, multiply the diameter by pi (π).

$c = \pi d$

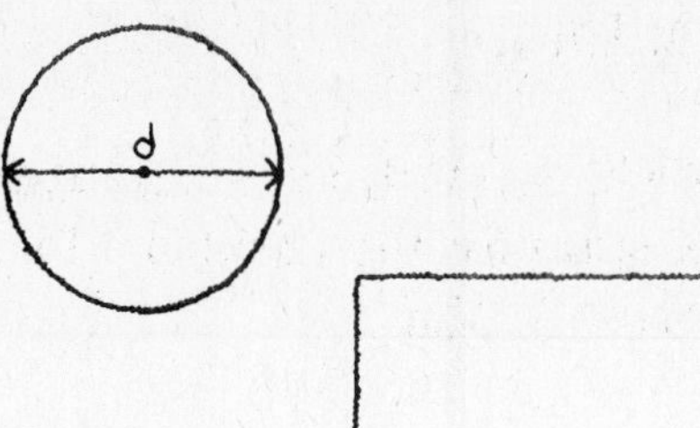

To find the perimeter of a

RECTANGLE, add twice the length to twice the width.

$p = 2l + 2w$

SQUARE, multiply the length of a side by 4.

$p = 4s$

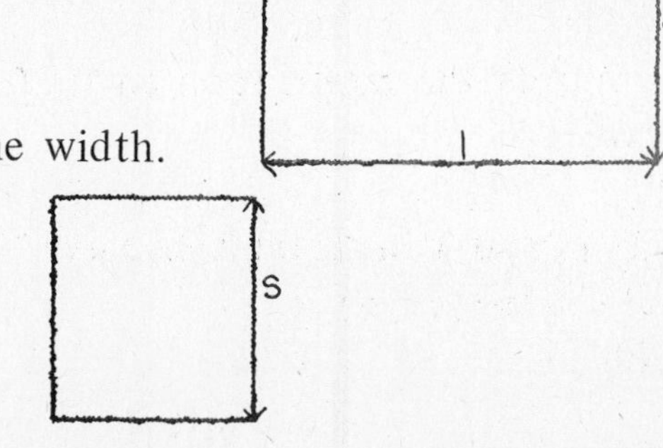

TRIANGLE, add the length of the sides.

$p = a + b + c$

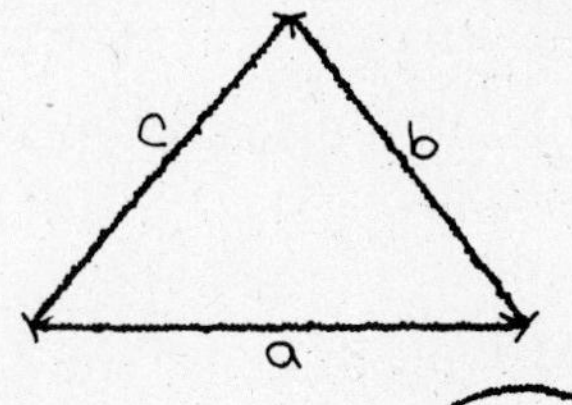

To find the area of a

CIRCLE, multiply the square of the radius by pi (π).

$A = \pi r^2$

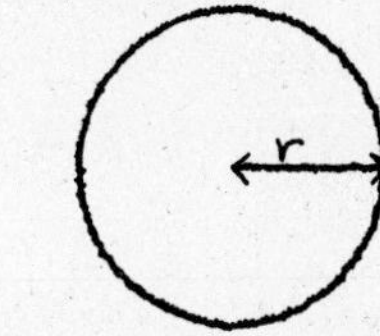

SQUARE, square one side.

$A = s^2$ or $A = s \times s$

RECTANGLE, multiply the base by the height.

$A = bh$

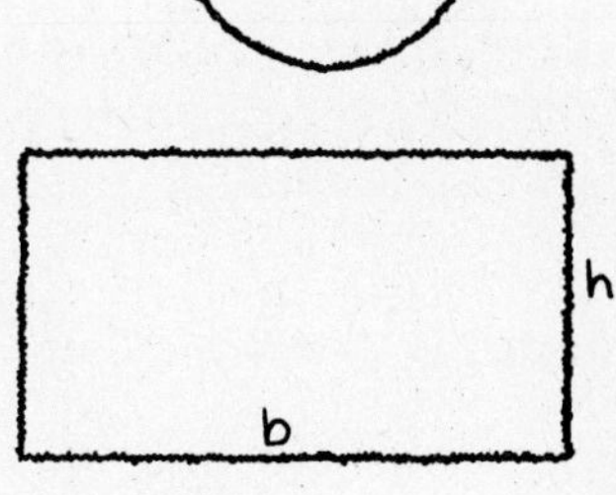

TRIANGLE, multiply the base by the height and divide by 2.

$A = \frac{1}{2}bh$ or $A = \frac{bh}{2}$

PARALLELOGRAM, multiply the base by the height.

$A = bh$

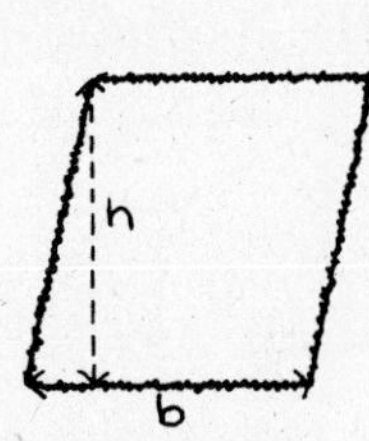

TRAPEZOID, multiply the sum of the lengths of the parallel sides by the height and divide by 2.

$A = h \times \frac{b^1 + b^2}{2}$

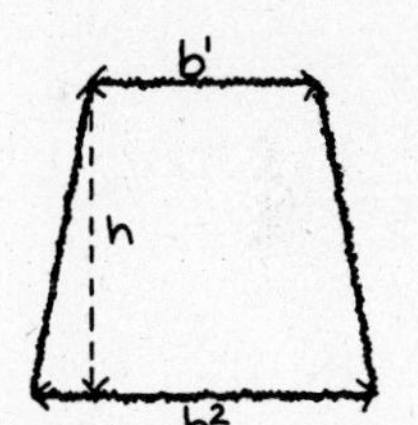

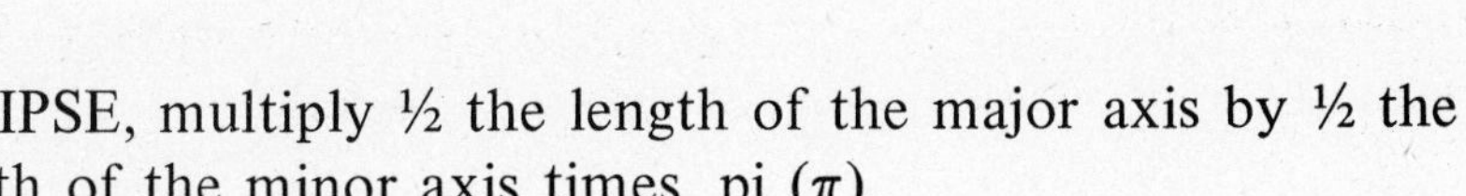

ELLIPSE, multiply ½ the length of the major axis by ½ the length of the minor axis times pi (π).

$A = \pi\ (\frac{1}{2}M \times \frac{1}{2}m)$

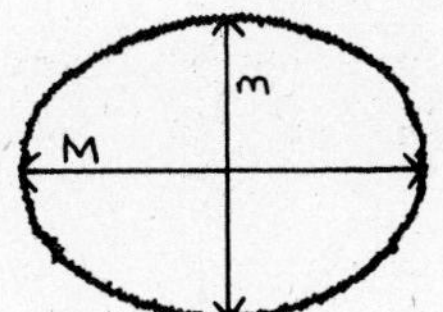

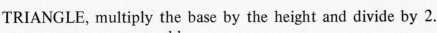

REGULAR POLYGON, multiply ½ the apothem (the perpendicular from the center to one side) by the number of sides times the length of a side.

$A = \frac{1}{2}ans$ or $A = \frac{1}{2}ap$

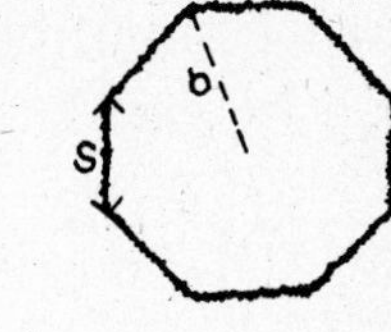

SPHERE, multiply the radius squared by 4 times pi (π).

$A = 4\pi r^2$

CYLINDER (lateral area or outside curved surface), multiply the diameter by the height times pi (π).

$A = \pi dh$

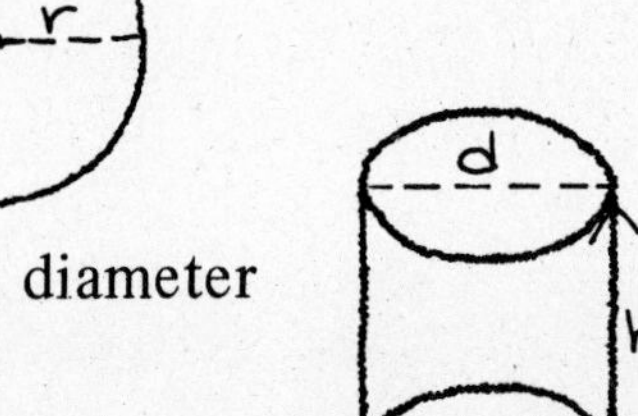

To find the total area of a

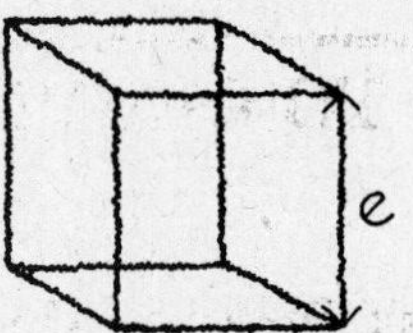

CUBE, square the length of one edge and multiply by 6.
$A = 6e^2$

RECTANGLE, add twice the product of the length and width, twice the product of the length and height, and twice the product of the width and height.
$A = 2lw + 2lh + 2wh$ or $A = 2(lw + lh + wh)$

CYLINDER, add the lateral area to the area of the two bases.

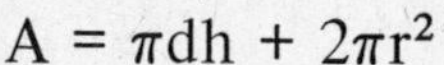

$A = \pi dh + 2\pi r^2$

To find the volume of a

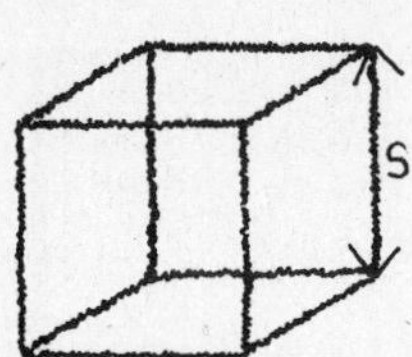

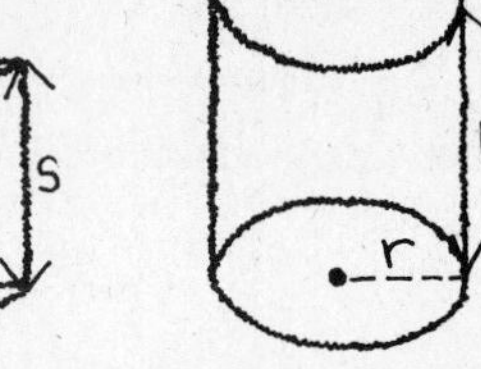

CUBE, cube the length of one side.
$V = s^3$

RECTANGULAR SOLID, multiply the length by the width times the height.
$V = lwh$

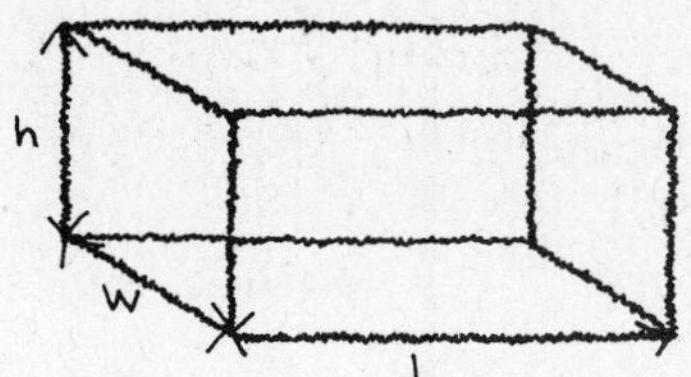

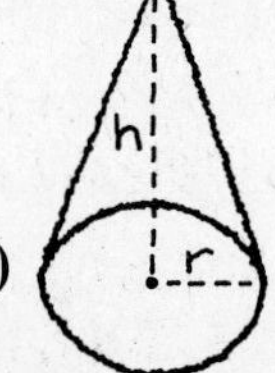

CONE, multiply the square of the radius of the base by the height times $\frac{1}{3}$ pi (π)
$V = \frac{1}{3}\pi r^2 h$

CYLINDER, multiply the square of the radius by the height times pi (π).
$V = \pi r^2 h$

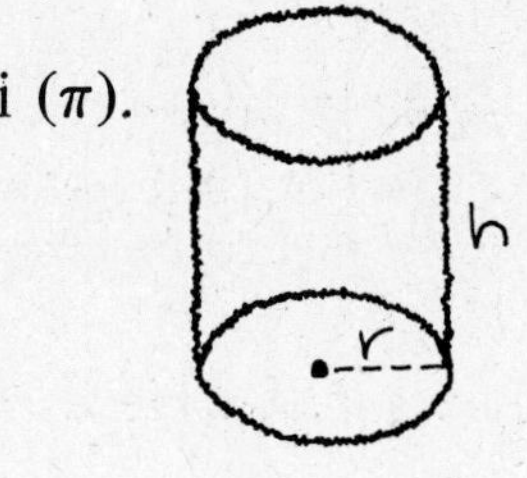

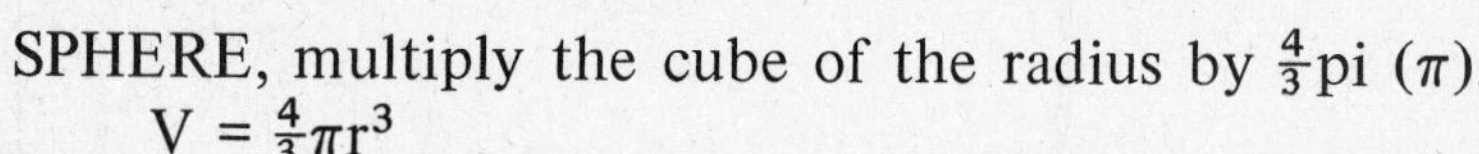

SPHERE, multiply the cube of the radius by $\frac{4}{3}$pi (π).
$V = \frac{4}{3}\pi r^3$

PYRAMID, multiply the area of the base by $\frac{1}{3}$ times the height.
$V = \frac{1}{3}bh$

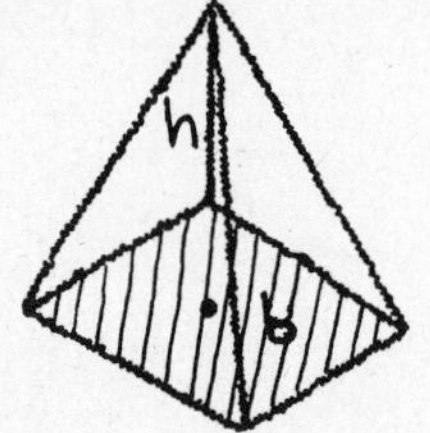

99 THINGS TO GRAPH AND SURVEY

Questions to ask for surveying and graphing

"How many . . . ?"

. . . people in your family
. . . rooms in your house
. . . light bulbs in your house
. . . cars in your family
. . . plants in your house
. . . televisions in your house
. . . electrical appliances in your house
. . . doors in your house
. . . windows in your house
. . . teeth do you have
. . . buttons do you have on
. . . pockets on what you're wearing
. . . relatives do you have
. . . letters in your name
. . . left- and right-handed people in your class

"At what time . . . ?"

. . . do you eat dinner
. . . do you get up
. . . do you go to bed
. . . do you leave for school
. . . do you get home from school
. . . is your favorite TV show on
. . . were you born

"How much time in a day or week do you spend . . . ?"

. . . watching television
. . . doing homework
. . . playing
. . . reading
. . . in a car or on a bus
. . . eating
. . . doing chores
. . . alone
. . . in activities such as Boy Scouts, Girl Scouts, piano lessons, etc.

"Who's your favorite . . . . ?"

. . . movie star
. . . TV star
. . . recording group
. . . book character
. . . sportsperson
. . . singer
. . . celebrity

"What's your favorite . . . . . . ?"

. . . ice cream flavor
. . . color
. . . TV program
. . . kind of car
. . . game or sport
. . . pet
. . . weather
. . . holiday
. . . film
. . . radio station
. . . food
. . . song
. . . number
. . . brand of jeans
. . . book
. . . animal
. . . building
. . . toy
. . . musical instrument
. . . pizza topping

"How many times in a day or week . . . ?"

. . . do you use the telephone
. . . do you drink water
. . . does the telephone ring

"How old do you think our teacher is?"
"What do you want to be when you grow up?"
"In which month were you born?"
"What is your zodiac sign?"
"Where do you shop for groceries?"
"How much is your weekly allowance?"
"What is the first number of your telephone number?"
"What is the last number of your telephone number?"
"How many times can you jump on one foot?"
"How many sit-ups (jumping jacks, push-ups, etc.) can you do?"
"How long can you talk (filibuster)?"
"How many times can you jump rope without missing?"
"How many times can you say 'toyboat' clearly and quickly?"

The following ideas for graphing require observation or measurement of other people and things.

Within a given population or area, graph the color of:

eyes
hair
shoes
articles of clothing
cars
flowers
books

Measure and graph people's:

heights
weights
length of arms, legs, or feet
circumference of heads

The following graphs generally can be done without interaction with other people.

Do weekly graphs of:

where people are eating lunch
students present or absent in class
the highest temperature for each day
the lowest temperature for each day

Do graphs at home of:

the kinds of silverware in a drawer
the kinds of dishes on a shelf
articles of clothing in a drawer or closet
types of TV commercials seen in an evening (cars, foods, cleaning products, etc.)

. . . And Other Things to Count and Graph

Choose a paragraph. Count and graph the number of times each letter of the alphabet appears in the paragraph.

Count and graph the number and kinds of P.E. equipment in your school.

Count and graph the number and kinds of supplies in your classroom (scissors, pencils, rulers, etc.).

Measure and graph the areas of all the rooms in your school.

Count and graph the number of times common names, such as Smith, Jones, Brown, White, Taylor, Johnson, Nelson, and Martin, appear in your telephone directory.

Count and graph the number of people in your class who have used each type of transportation: bus, airplane, taxi, ferry, train, horse, etc.

PART **3**

PEOPLE AND ANIMALS

eight
PEOPLE

"HAIL TO THE CHIEF"—U.S. PRESIDENTS

President	Date of Birth	Date of Death	Date of Inauguration
George Washington	Feb. 22, 1732	Dec. 14, 1799	Apr. 30, 1789
John Adams	Oct. 30, 1735	July 4, 1826	Mar. 4, 1797*
Thomas Jefferson	Apr. 13, 1743	July 4, 1826	1801
James Madison	Mar. 16, 1751	June 28, 1836	1809
James Monroe	Apr. 28, 1758	July 4, 1831	1817
John Quincy Adams	July 11, 1767	Feb. 23, 1848	1825
Andrew Jackson	Mar. 15, 1767	June 8, 1845	1829
Martin Van Buren	Dec. 5, 1782	July 24, 1862	1837
William Henry Harrison	Feb. 9, 1773	Apr. 4, 1841	1841
John Tyler	Mar. 29, 1790	Jan. 18, 1862	1841 (April 6, after Harrison's death)
James Knox Polk	Nov. 2, 1795	June 15, 1849	1845
Zachary Taylor	Nov. 24, 1784	July 9, 1850	1849 (March 5)
Millard Fillmore	Jan. 7, 1800	Mar. 8, 1874	1850 (July 10, after Taylor's death)
Franklin Pierce	Nov. 23, 1804	Oct. 8, 1869	1853
James Buchanan	Apr. 23, 1791	June 1, 1868	1857
Abraham Lincoln	Feb. 12, 1809	Apr. 15, 1865	1861
Andrew Johnson	Dec. 29, 1808	July 31, 1875	1865 (April 15, after Lincoln's death)

Ulysses S. Grant	Apr. 27, 1822	July 23, 1885	1869
Rutherford B. Hayes	Oct. 4, 1822	Jan. 17, 1893	1877
James A. Garfield	Nov. 19, 1831	Sept. 19, 1881	1881
Chester A. Arthur	Oct. 5, 1829	Nov. 18, 1886	1881 (Sept. 20, after Garfield's death)
Grover Cleveland	Mar. 18, 1837	June 24, 1908	1885
Benjamin Harrison	Aug. 20, 1833	Mar. 13, 1901	1889
Grover Cleveland	Mar. 18, 1837	June 24, 1908	1893
William McKinley	Jan. 29, 1843	Sept. 14, 1901	1897
Theodore Roosevelt	Oct. 27, 1858	Jan. 6, 1919	1901 (Sept. 14, after McKinley's death
William H. Taft	Sept. 15, 1857	Mar. 8, 1930	1909
Woodrow Wilson	Dec. 28, 1856	Feb. 3, 1924	1913
Warren G. Harding	Nov. 2, 1865	Aug. 2, 1923	1921
Calvin Coolidge	July 4, 1872	Jan. 5, 1933	1923 (Aug. 3, after Harding's death)
Herbert Hoover	Aug. 10, 1874	Oct. 20, 1964	1929
Franklin D. Roosevelt	Jan. 30, 1882	Apr. 12, 1945	1933
Harry S. Truman	May 8, 1884	Dec. 26, 1972	1945 (April 12, after Roosevelt's death)
Dwight D. Eisenhower	Oct. 14, 1890	Mar. 28, 1969	Jan. 20, 1953
John F. Kennedy	May 29, 1917	Nov. 22, 1963	Jan. 20, 1961
Lyndon B. Johnson	Aug. 27, 1908	Jan. 22, 1973	Nov. 22, 1963 (after Kennedy's death)
Richard M. Nixon	Jan. 9, 1913		Jan. 20, 1969
Gerald R. Ford	July 14, 1913		Aug. 9, 1974
Jimmy Carter	Oct. 1, 1924		Jan. 20, 1977

*The following inaugurations were also on Mar. 4–through 1933, unless otherwise noted.

Presidential Activities

1. Make a list of the Presidents' ages when they died. (Pay special attention to the months.)
2. Make a list of the Presidents' ages when they were inaugurated. (Pay special attention to the months.)
3. Rearrange the list of Presidents to read in alphabetical order.

4. Group the Presidents according to the months in which they were born or died.
5. Group the Presidents according to the number of terms to which they were elected.
6. Make a list of facts—such as the President with the longest life, shortest life, shortest term of office, longest term of office, youngest to become President, and oldest to become President.
7. Add other columns to the chart, such as Vice-Presidents, previous professions or occupations, and party affiliations.
8. Do research to find out about:

   a. world events that occurred during a President's term of office;
   b. important legislation passed during a President's term of office;
   c. a President's early life.

WOMEN

This is a representative list of women who have made contributions in various fields.

Jane Addams—American social worker and humanitarian

Louisa May Alcott—American writer; author of *Little Women*

Judith Anderson—stage actress

Marian Anderson—American opera singer; first black to sing with the Metropolitan Opera Company

Susan B. Anthony—reformer and leader in the American women's suffrage movement

Joan Baez—American folk singer; active in antiwar and civil rights movements of the 1960s

Sirimavo Bandaranaike—world's first female prime minister (of Sri Lanka)

Romana Acosta Bañuelos—treasurer of the U.S., 1971–1974

Clara Barton—founded the American Red Cross

Simone de Beauvoir—French author

Catharine Beecher—early supporter of education for women

Patty Berg—a top tournament winner in women's golf

Sarah Bernhardt—American actress

Mary McLeod Bethune—American educator who worked to improve educational opportunities for blacks

Nellie Bly (Elizabeth Cochrane Seaman)–American journalist

Evangeline Booth–first woman to become international leader and general of the Salvation Army

Belle Boyd–Confederate spy

Sophonisba Breckinridge–pioneer teacher of Social Work

Emily Brontë–English novelist

Elizabeth Barrett Browning–a poet of Victorian England

Pearl S. Buck–American author

St. Frances Xavier Cabrini–first (naturalized) U.S. citizen to become a saint

Calamity Jane (Martha Jane Canary)–American frontierswoman

Mary Steichen Calderone–American physician

Maria Callas–American operatic soprano

Rachel Carson–American marine biologist and science writer

Mary Cassatt–American painter

Carrie Chapman Catt–American leader in the campaign for woman suffrage; founded what has become the League of Women Voters

Chicang Ch'ing–wife of Mao Tse-tung; became Chinese leader after Mao's death for a brief period

Shirley Chisholm–first black woman in U.S. Congress; campaigned for 1972 Presidential nomination

Jacqueline Cochran–American businesswoman and pioneer airplane pilot

Colette (Sidonie Gabrielle Claudine)–French author

Charlotte Corday–French patriot during the French Revolution

Marie Curie–Nobel Prize winning French physicist

Bette Davis–American motion-picture actress

Paulina Davis–American social reformer for women's rights

Agnes De Mille–American choreographer, dancer, and author

Bernadette Devlin–civil rights leader of the Roman Catholic minority in Northern Ireland

Babe Didrikson–one of the greatest of woman athletes

Dorothea Dix–led movement to build state hospitals for the mentally ill in the U.S.

Daphne du Maurier–British novelist

Isadora Duncan–greatly influential in the American dance of the early 1900s

Jacqueline du Pré–English cellist

Amelia Earhart–American aviator, writer, and lecturer; one of the first women pilots in the U.S.

Mary Baker Eddy–founder of Christian Science and the Church of Christ, Scientists

George Eliot (Mary Ann Evans)–great English novelist

Edna Ferber–American novelist and playwright

Margot Fonteyn–great English ballerina

Betty Friedan–American author and one of the founders of women's liberation movement

Indira Gandhi–first woman prime minister of India

Judy Garland–American singer and motion-picture actress

Emma Goldman–came to the U.S. from Russia; lectured in favor of anarchism and women's rights

Martha Graham–American pioneer of modern dance; dancer and choreographer

Ella T. Grasso–first woman elected governor in the U.S. who did not succeed her husband in the office

Kate Greenaway–English illustrator of children's books

Angelina and Sara Grimké–sisters who became abolitionists and pioneers in the U.S. women's rights movement

Alice Hamilton–American physician; did pioneer work in industrial medicine

Patricia Roberts Harris–first black woman to serve as U.S. ambassador

Helen Hayes–American stage and screen actress

Lillian Hellman–American playwright

Carla Anderson Hills–Secretary of Housing and Urban Development under President Ford

Billie Holiday–American jazz singer

Julia Ward Howe–American writer, lecturer, social reformer

Helen Hunt Jackson–worked for American Indian rights

Irène Joliot-Curie–Nobel Prize winner for chemistry; Marie Curie's daughter

Helen Keller–overcame physical handicaps (unable to see and hear) to become internationally famous; helped thousands of handicapped persons lead fuller lives

Elizabeth Kenny (Sister Kenny)–Australian nurse who developed a special method of treating polio

Billie Jean King–American tennis star

Selma Lagerlöf–Swedish writer; won the Nobel prize for literature in 1909

Lotte Lehmann–German soprano

Belva Lockwood–American reformer and women's suffrage leader

Juliette Gordon Low–founded the Girl Scouts in America

Amy Lowell–American poet and critic

Clare Boothe Luce–first woman to represent the U.S. in a major diplomatic post

Mary McCarthy–American author

Carson McCullers–American novelist

Golda Meir–prime minister of Israel, 1969–1974

Edna St. Vincent Millay–American poet

Marianne Moore–American poet

Grandma Moses (Anna Mary Roberson Moses)–American primitive painter

Lucretia Mott–American reformer; worked for women's rights and the abolition of slavery

Carry Amelia Moore Nation–crusaded against the use of alcoholic beverages

Florence Nightingale–founder of the modern nursing profession

Annie Oakley–American markswoman

Georgia O'Keeffe–American artist

Ruth Bryan Owen–first American woman to represent the U.S. in a foreign country

Vijaya Lakshmi Pandit–Indian woman famous for work in government and the women's movement

Dorothy Parker–American poet and writer of short stories and literary criticism

Frances Perkins–first woman cabinet member of the U.S.

Mary Pickford–American movie actress and producer

Sylvia Plath–American poet

Katherine Anne Porter–American writer, famous for her short stories

Leontyne Price–American operatic soprano

Jeannette Rankin–first woman elected to the U.S. Congress

Mary Roberts Rinehart–American novelist and playwright

Eleanor Roosevelt–wife of Franklin Delano Roosevelt; she became prominent in her own right for her humanitarian work

Nellie Tayloe Ross–first woman governor of the U.S.

Ruth Saint Denis–American dancer, teacher, and choreographer

George Sand (Amantine Dupin)–French novelist

Dorothy Sayers–English author, famous for detective stories

Elizabeth Ann Seton–first native-born person in the U.S. to be recognized as a saint

Beverly Sills–American opera singer

Gertrude Stein–American author

Gloria Steinem–American writer and leading supporter of women's liberation movement

Harriet Beecher Stowe–American novelist and writer

Joan Sutherland–Australian operatic soprano

Maria Tallchief–American ballerina

Helen Brooke Taussig–American physician specializing in children's heart diseases; discovered the cause of bluish tinge in skin of "blue babies"

Balentina Vladimirova Tereshkova–Russian woman who became the first woman to travel in space

Margaret Thatcher–first woman to head a British political party

Sojourner Truth (Isabella Baumfree)–American abolitionist; first black woman orator to speak out against slavery

Harriet Tubman–black American who helped hundreds of slaves escape to freedom; most famous leader of the underground railroad

Sigrid Undset–Norwegian author

Jane Goodall-Van Lawick–English zoologist; became famous for behavior studies of chimpanzees

Laura Ingalls Wilder–American author of children's books

Emma Willard–first American woman to lead movement for higher education for women

Frances E. Willard–American educator and social reformer

Victoria C. Woodhull–first woman to run for President of the U.S.

EXPLORERS AND DISCOVERERS

c. 1000	Leif Ericson	Thought to be the first European to reach North American mainland
1487–1488	Bartolomeu Dias	First European to sail around the Cape of Good Hope in Africa
1492–1504	Christopher Columbus	Made voyages to West Indies and Caribbean Islands
1497–1498	John Cabot	Made voyages across the Atlantic to the Canadian coast
1498	Vasco da Gama	First European to reach India by sea (sailed around Africa)
1497–1503	Amerigo Vespucci	Made voyages to West Indies and South America
1513	Vasco Núñez de Balboa	Crossed Isthmus of Panama; sighted Pacific Ocean
1513	Juan Ponce de León	Explored Florida
1519–1521	Hernando Cortes	Explored and conquered Mexico
1519–1521	Ferdinand Magellan	Led first voyage around the world; proved the world is round
1524	Giovanni da Verrazano	Explored Atlantic coast of the Americas while searching for a Northwest Passage

1531–1535	Francisco Pizarro	Explored and conquered Peru
1535	Jacques Cartier	Discovered and sailed up St. Lawrence River
1539–1542	Hernando de Soto	Explored Southeastern U.S.; reached Mississippi River
1540–1542	Francisco V. de Coronado	Explored Southwestern U.S., as far as central Kansas
1541	Francisco de Orellana	Explored Amazon River
1577–1580	Sir Francis Drake	First Englishman to sail around the world; explored California coast
1603–1616	Samuel de Champlain	Explored eastern coast of North America and St. Lawrence River
1609–1611	Henry Hudson	Explored Hudson Bay and River area
1673	Louis Joliet and Jacques Marquette	Explored northern Mississippi River basin
1727–1729	Vitus Bering	Explored Bering Strait; discovered Alaska
1768–1779	James Cook	Made extensive explorative voyages in the South Pacific
1789–1793	Sir Alexander Mackenzie	Explored western Canada
1804–1806	William Clark and Meriwether Lewis	Led expedition across the Rocky Mountains to the Pacific Ocean and back
1842–1846	John Charles Frémont	Explored extensively in western U.S.
1849–1873	David Livingstone	Greatest European explorer of Africa
1853–1858	Sir Richard Burton	Explored Arabia and East Africa
1874–1889	Sir Henry Stanley	Proved the source of the Nile; explored Congo River
1909	Robert Peary	Led the first expedition that reached the North Pole
1911	Roald Amundsen	First to reach the South Pole
1926–1929	Richard E. Byrd	Flew over both the North and South Poles; led five expeditions into the Antarctic
1957–1958	Sir Vivian Fuchs	Led first expedition across Antarctica

INVENTIONS AND INVENTORS

Thomas Edison is said to be the greatest of all the inventors in history. Among his many inventions and developments (he received 1,093 patents) are the electric light, a mimeograph machine, a motion-picture camera and projector, and the phonograph. We selected the following inventions because they are familiar products known by most children.

airplane, the first successful–Orville and Wilbur Wright 1903

aspirin–Dresser 1889

bakelite–one of the first plastics–L. H. Baekeland 1907

balloons that carry people in the air–Montgolfier 1783

bicycle, modern type–James Starley 1884

bifocal lens–Benjamin Franklin 1780

carpet sweeper–Bissell 1876

cellophane–J. E. Brandenberger 1912

clock, pendulum type–Christian Huygens 1657

dynamite–Alfred Nobel 1866

elevator, power type–Elisha Otis 1852

food preservation, by canning–Appert 1810

food preservation, by freezing–Clarence Birdseye 1920s

helicopter–Igor Sikorsky 1939

hydroplane–Glenn Curtiss 1911

kodak, roll-film hand camera–Eastman and Walker 1888

lawn mower–A. M. Hills 1868

lightning rod–Benjamin Franklin 1752

locomotive, first successful steam–George Stephenson 1829

mason jar–J. Mason 1858

matches, friction–John Walker 1827

microphone–Emil Berliner 1877

microscope, compound–Zacharias Janssen 1590

nylon–E. I. du Pont de Nemours & Co. 1937

oleomargarine–H. Mege-Mouries 1869

pen, first successful fountain–L. E. Waterman 1884

penicillin–Alexander Fleming 1929

phonograph–Thomas Edison 1877

piano–Bartollomeo Cristofori 1709

polio vaccines–Jonas Salk (1953) and Albert Sabin (1955)

printing from movable type–Johann Gutenberg 1450

rabies vaccine–Louis Pasteur 1885

radar–A. Hoyt Taylor and Leo C. Young 1922

razor, safety–Gillette 1895; electric–Schick 1931

refrigerating machine–John Gorie 1851

revolver–Samuel Colt 1835

sewing machine–Elias Howe 1846

telegraph—Samuel Morse 1837

telephone—Alexander Graham Bell 1876

television—J. L. Baird 1925; independently by C. F. Jenkins 1925

thermometer—Galileo 1593; mercury thermometer—Gabriel Fahrenheit 1714

typewriter, first practicable—C. L. Sholes 1865

vacuum bottle—James Dewar 1893

vulcanization of rubber, a process that made rubber useful by giving it elasticity, hardness, and strength—Charles Goodyear 1844

x-ray—Wilhelm Roentgen 1895

zipper—Judson 1891

AWARDS FOR STUDENTS

Everybody likes recognition, so end your year with an Awards Day. Here's a list of awards that may match some of the personalities in your class. Obviously, some of the awards are stated with tongue in cheek, and need to be given and received with a sense of humor. The important thing is that everyone gets an award.

THE CHEERLEADER AWARD to the most enthusiastic

THE CHESHIRE CAT AWARD to the person with the biggest smile

THE NEATEST DESK or CUBBY AWARD

THE CALLIGRAPHY AWARD to the person with the neatest handwriting

THE VAN GOGH AWARD to the best artist

THE MOST HELPFUL AWARD

THE DR. FEELGOOD AWARD to the person with the best attendance

THE THESAURUS AWARD to the person with the biggest vocabulary

THE FUNK AND WAGNALL AWARD to the best speller

THE FASHION PLATE AWARD to the best dressed

THE PHILANTHROPIC AWARD to the most generous

THE UMP AWARD to the best referee

THE SPIC AND SPAN AWARD to the best cleaner-upper

THE BEST SECRETARY AWARD

THE BEST EXCUSE-MAKER AWARD

THE MOST LOQUACIOUS AWARD

THE LADY GODIVA AWARD to the person with the longest hair

THE LONGEST LEGS AWARD

THE LITERARY AWARD to the person who has read the most books

THE BETTER-LATE-THAN-NEVER AWARD

THE ATHLETE AWARD

THE "I DIDN'T DO IT" AWARD to the person who is good at denying things

THE LOST AND FOUND AWARD to the person who is always losing things

THE "WE TRY HARDER" AWARD

THE STICK WITH IT AWARD to the person who stays with a task

THE SOFTEST-SPOKEN AWARD

THE LOUDEST-SPOKEN AWARD

THE HERMES AWARD to the best messenger

THE DO-RE-MI AWARD to the best singer

THE DEAN OF THE DISCOS AWARD to the best dancer

THE STAND-UP COMIC AWARD to the best joke teller

THE BIGGEST NAGGER AWARD

THE EASY-GOING AWARD to the most agreeable

THE BULL IN THE CHINA SHOP AWARD to the clumsiest

THE IMPOUND AWARD to the person who has lost the most stuff to the teacher's desk

THE BEST AFTER-SCHOOL TEACHER'S CAR LOADER or UNLOADER

THE TURTLE AWARD to the person who gets things done slowly

THE ALBERT EINSTEIN AWARD for outstanding achievement in science

THE ALWAYS ROOM FOR ONE MORE AWARD to the person with the fullest desk or cubby

THE NUMERO UNO AWARD to the best mathematician

THE "I'LL DO IT" AWARD to the person who volunteers the most

THE KVETCH AWARD to the biggest complainer

THE WORK IS NOT GOOD FOR MY HEALTH AWARD to the person who tries to avoid all assignments

THE EXTRA CREDIT AWARD

THE SIDE-BY-SIDE AWARD to two people who are inseparable

THE PEACEMAKER AWARD

THE GIGGLER AWARD

THE "I'D RATHER DO IT MYSELF" AWARD to the most independent

THE MOST SERIOUS AWARD

THE MOST IMPROVED AWARD

PEOPLE CELEBRATE—ETHNIC HOLIDAYS

Although some of the holidays on this list are celebrated by many Americans, we have listed the ethnic group for which the holiday holds special significance. Religious holidays have generally been omitted.

Date	Name	Ethnic Group	
January 15	Martin Luther King, Jr. Day	Black American	Commemorates the birthday of Martin Luther King, Jr., civil rights leader.
Observed between Jan. 21 & Feb. 19	Chinese New Year's	Chinese	Celebration lasts several days, ending with festivities that include a parade featuring the Golden Dragon, gongs, drums, and firecrackers.
February 4	Kosciuszko Day	Polish	Honors the birthday of Tadeusz Kosciuszko, who fought with the colonists in the American Revolutionary War.
March 3	Hina Matsuri (Girl's Day)	Japanese	Festival honoring girls and their dolls. Traditional dolls are displayed in the home.

March 17	St. Patrick's Day	Irish	Feast day of St. Patrick, patron saint of Ireland. Celebrated with parades, balls, dinners.
March–April (date varies)	Pesach (Passover)	Jewish	Feast of unleavened bread. Commemorates the deliverance of the Jews from Egypt; observed for eight days.
May 5	Cinco de Mayo	Mexican	Commemorates the defeat of the French at the Battle of Puebla in 1867. Celebrated with a fiesta.
May 5	Tango No Sekku (Boy's Day)	Japanese	Festival honoring boys. Carp kites symbolizing strength and determination are flown from rooftops.
May 17	Syttende Mai	Norwegian	Celebrates the adoption of the Norwegian constitution in 1814.
June 24	Swedish Midsummer Festival	Swedish	Celebrated with dancing and the raising of the maypole.
July 29	Olsok Eve Festival (frequently called Norway Day in U.S.)	Norwegian	Commemorates the death of St. Olaf, the martyr king Olav Haraldsson who brought Christianity to Norway.
Setpember 27 (observed on the 4th Friday of September)	American Indian Day	American Indian	Honors native Americans.
September 28	Cabrillo Day	Portuguese	Six-day festival observed in California honoring Juan Rodriguez Cabrillo, Portuguese navigator who discovered California on September 28, 1542.
September (date varies)	Rosh Hashanah	Jewish	Jewish New Year
October 9	Leif Ericson Day	Norwegian & Icelandic	Commemorates the landing of Norsemen in Vinland, New England about A.D. 1000.
October 11	Pulaski Memorial Day	Polish	Commemorates the death of General Casimir Pulaski, hero of the American Revolution.
October 12 (observed on 2nd Monday of October)	Columbus Day	Italian	Commemorates the sighting of San Salvador on October 12, 1492, by Christopher Columbus.

BUTCHER, BAKER, CANDLESTICK MAKER—PEOPLE'S JOBS

A acrobat, actor, aircraft worker, airline worker, architect, artist, assembler, astrologer, athlete, attorney, auctioneer, auto mechanic

B babysitter, baker, banker, bank teller, bartender, beautician, beekeeper, biologist, bookkeeper, brick mason, broadcaster, bus driver, butcher, buyer

C cake decorator, calligrapher, carpenter, cashier, chauffeur, chef, chemist, choreographer, clerk, computer programmer, contractor, construction worker, controller, cook

D dancer, data processor, dental hygienist, dentist, dermatologist, designer, dietician, disc jockey, draftsperson, drummer

E ecologist, economist, editor, electrician, engineer, engraver, entertainer, estimator

F factory worker, farmer, file clerk, filmmaker, fireman, fisherman, florist, fortune teller

G gardener, genealogist, geologist, ghost writer, golfer, graphic artist, grocer, guard

H hair stylist, handyman, horse trainer, hypnotist

I ice skater, illustrator, innkeeper, inspector, instructor, insurance agent, interior decorator, interpreter, inventor, inventory control clerk, investigator

J janitor, jeweler, judge

K keypunch operator

L laboratory technician, legal secretary, librarian, linguist, lithographer, loan officer, locksmith

M machinist, mail carrier, manager, manicurist, masseur or masseuse, mechanic, medical assistant, metallurgist, meteorologist, milliner, model, musician

N news reporter, numismatist, nurse, nurseryman

O occupational therapist, oil worker, optometrist, order clerk, organist

P painter, personnel worker, pharmacist, photographer, physical therapist, physician, piano tuner, pilot, plasterer, plumber, police officer, printer, purchasing agent

Q quality control manager, quilt maker

R railroad worker, rancher, realtor, receptionist, recreation director, refinisher, repair person, restaurateur, roofer

S salesperson, scuba diver, seamstress, secretary, service man or woman (Army, Navy, etc.), shipping clerk, sign painter, social worker, stenographer, steward or stewardess, surveyor

T tailor, tattooer, taxidermist, taxi driver, teacher, telephone operator, therapist, tool and die maker, travel agent, truck driver, typesetter, typist

U undertaker, upholsterer, urban planner

V valet, veterinarian, video technician

W waiter or waitress, warehouse person, watchmaker, welder, winemaker, writer

X Xerox operator, x-ray technician, xmas tree grower

Y yoga instructor

Z zoologist

Activities With People's Jobs

1. Write verbs to describe what each worker does.
2. Use the workers listed in one letter category for the characters in a story. Some examples of titles are: "The Butler Did It," using the workers in the B list, and "The Plumber's Helpers," using the workers in the P list as characters.
3. List the workers within general categories, such as Office, Entertainment, Industry, or Workers Who Come to Your Home.
4. Choose one or more of the following "Planned Communities" and list all the workers who might live there: Beauty Burg, Fix-it Ville, Healthy Hamlet, Food Farm, Sports Spa, and Number Town.
5. Use the list and another source, such as the newspaper want ads, to find all the different kinds of mechanics, computer workers, engineers, doctors, designers, artists, inspectors, managers, reporters, clerks, supervisors, technicians, and writers.

TEAMS OF MAJOR U.S. SPORTS

Baseball

Atlanta Braves
Baltimore Orioles
Boston Red Sox
California Angels
Chicago Cubs
Chicago White Sox
Cincinnati Reds
Cleveland Indians
Detroit Tigers
Houston Astros
Kansas City Royals
Los Angeles Dodgers
Milwaukee Brewers
Minnesota Twins
Montreal Expos
New York Mets
New York Yankees
Oakland A's
Philadelphia Phillies
Pittsburgh Pirates
St. Louis Cardinals
San Diego Padres
San Francisco Giants
Texas Rangers

Basketball

Atlanta Hawks
Boston Celtics
Chicago Bulls
Cleveland Cavaliers
Denver Nuggets
Detroit Pistons
Golden State Warriors
Houston Rockets
Indiana Pacers
Kansas City Kings
Los Angeles Lakers
Milwaukee Bucks
New Jersey Nets
New Orleans Jazz
New York Knickerbockers
Philadelphia 76er's
Phoenix Suns
Portland Trailblazers
San Antonio Spurs
San Diego Clippers
Seattle SuperSonics
Washington Bullets

Football

Atlanta Falcons
Baltimore Colts
Buffalo Bills
Chicago Bears
Cincinnati Bengals
Cleveland Browns
Dallas Cowboys
Denver Broncos
Detroit Lions
Green Bay Packers
Houston Oilers
Kansas City Chiefs
Los Angeles Rams
Miami Dolphins
Minnesota Vikings
New England Patriots
New Orleans Saints
New York Giants
New York Jets
Oakland Raiders
Philadelphia Eagles
Pittsburgh Steelers
St. Louis Cardinals
San Diego Chargers
San Francisco 49er's
Seattle Seahawks
Tampa Bay Buccaneers
Washington Redskins

Hockey

Atlanta Flames
Birmingham Bulls
Boston Bruins
Buffalo Sabres
Calgary Cowboys
Chicago Black Hawks
Cincinnati Stingers
Cleveland Barons
Colorado Rockies
Detroit Red Wings
Edmonton Oilers
Houston Aeros
Indianapolis Racers
Los Angeles Kings
Minnesota Fighting Saints
Minnesota North Stars
Montreal Canadiens
New England Whalers
New York Islanders
New York Rangers
Philadelphia Flyers
Phoenix Roadrunners
Pittsburgh Penguins
Quebec Nordiques
St. Louis Blues
San Diego Mariners
Toronto Maple Leafs
Vancouver Canucks
Washington Capitals
Winnipeg Jets

MODERN OLYMPIC GAMES—DATES AND LOCATIONS

The first modern Olympics in 1896 had nine nations represented. Today more than one hundred nations send athletes to compete.

Summer Games		Winter Games	
1896	Athens, Greece		
1900	Paris, France		
1904	St. Louis, Missouri, U.S.A.		
1906	Athens, Greece (unofficial)		
1908	London, England		
1912	Stockholm, Sweden		
1920	Antwerp, Belgium		
1924	Paris, France	1924	Chamonix, France
1928	Amsterdam, Netherlands	1928	St. Moritz, Switzerland
1932	Los Angeles, California, U.S.A.	1932	Lake Placid, New York, U.S.A.
1936	Berlin, Germany	1936	Garmisch-Partenkirchen, Germany
1948	London, England	1948	St. Moritz, Switzerland
1952	Helsinki, Finland	1952	Oslo, Norway
1956	Melbourne, Australia	1956	Cortina d'Ampezzo, Italy
1960	Rome, Italy	1960	Squaw Valley, California, U.S.A.
1964	Tokyo, Japan	1964	Innsbruck, Austria
1968	Mexico City, Mexico	1968	Grenoble, France
1972	Munich, Germany	1972	Sapporo, Japan
1976	Montreal, Canada	1976	Innsbruck, Austria
1980	Scheduled for Moscow, U.S.S.R.	1980	Scheduled for Lake Placid, New York, U.S.A.

ONESIES, TWOSIES–JACKS GAMES

These games were written for right-handers. The instructions can be reversed for left-handed players, and can be played through to "twosies," "threesies," etc.

Around the World

onesies: Throw the ball up and pick up a jack. Before catching the ball, circle the ball clockwise with your hand, ending underneath the ball to catch it. Put the jacks in your left hand.

Bouncing Babies

onesies: Throw the ball up with your left hand. Pick up a jack with your right hand, then catch the ball with your left hand. The ball must be caught after you pick up the jack.

Breaking Eggs ("Knocksies")

onesies: Throw the ball up, pick up a jack, knock it on the floor once, and put it in your left hand. Then catch the ball before it bounces more than once.

Flying Dutchman

onesies: Throw the ball up, pick up a jack, catch the ball in your right hand before it bounces more than once. Hold the ball back on your palm and the jack forward on your fingers and toss both into the air. Catch the jack in your left hand, let the ball bounce once before you catch it in your right hand.

Picking Cherries (Cherries in the Basket)

onesies: Throw the ball up, pick up a jack, and put it in your left hand (the basket). Then catch the ball in your right hand before it bounces more than once.

Pigs in the Pen

Form the pen by cupping your left hand and putting it down with the side of your little finger and the side of your thumb lying flat on the floor. The pen may not be moved until you have completed a series (onesies, twosies, etc.).

onesies: Throw the ball up and, with your right hand, slide one jack into the pen. Then catch the ball before it bounces more than once.

Sheep Over the Fence

Make the fence by placing the side of your left hand perpendicular to the floor. This fence may not be moved until you have completed a series (onesies, twosies, etc.).

onesies: Throw the ball up, pick up one jack, and put it on the other side of the "fence." Then catch the ball with your right hand before it bounces more than once.

Shooting Stars

onesies: Throw the ball up, pick up a jack, and catch the ball with your right hand before it bounces more than once. Hold the ball back on the palm of your hand with your thumb and leave the jack forward on your fingers. Toss the jack up about 6 inches in the air and catch it with your left hand.

Adapted from Marta Weigle, *Jacks and Jack Games: Follow My Fancy* (New York: Dover, 1970).

JUMP ROPE RHYMES

Add to the children's jump rope repertoire with these jump rope rhymes. Make use of them in another way by charting the rhymes and putting them on a Copycat Rack. Since many children like having their own copies, they will enjoy copying the rhymes for handwriting practice. Some other fun things to copy are recipes, song lyrics, and jokes.

Down by the ocean,
Down by the sea,
Johnny broke a milk bottle
And blamed it on me.
I told Ma and Ma told Pa,
Johnny got a lickin'
Ha! Ha! Ha!
How many lickin's did he get?
1, 2, 3, ...

John and Mary up in a tree,
K-I-S-S-I-N-G
First comes love,
Then comes marriage,
Here comes Mary
With a baby carriage.

I'm a little Dutch girl dressed in blue,
Here are the things I like to do:
Salute to the captain, bow to the queen,
Turn my back on the naughty, naughty king.
I can do the tap dance, I can do the split,
I can do the holka polka, just like this.
1, 2, 3, ...

Ice cream soda,
Delaware punch,
Tell me the initials
Of your honeybunch.
A, B, C, D, E . . . . . .

Cinderella dressed in yellow,
Went upstairs to see her fellow.
How many kisses did she get?
1, 2, 3, ...

Cinderella dressed in yellow,
Went upstairs to kiss her fellow.
By mistake, she kissed a snake.
How many doctors did it take?
1, 2, 3, ...

Anna Banana
Played the piana.
All she knew was the Star Spangled Banner.
She wiggles, she waggles,
And does the split,
And when she misses, she misses like this.

My mother, your mother, live across the way,
Three sixteen, East Broadway.
Every time they have a fight, this what they say:
Lady, lady turn around,
Lady, lady touch the ground,
Lady, lady show your shoes,
Lady, lady out goes YOU.

Policeman, policeman
Do your duty,
Here comes (name of person),
The American beauty.
She can do the rhumba,
She can do the splits,
She can wear her skirts
Up over her hips.

Teddy Bear, Teddy Bear, turn around,
Teddy Bear, Teddy Bear, touch the ground.
Teddy Bear, Teddy Bear, tie your shoes,
Teddy Bear, Teddy Bear, read the news.
Teddy Bear, Teddy Bear, go upstairs,
Teddy Bear, Teddy Bear, say your prayers.
Teddy Bear, Teddy Bear, turn out the light,
Teddy Bear, Teddy Bear, say goodnight.

Mother, Mother, I am ill,
Call for the doctor over the hill.
In comes the doctor,
In comes the nurse,
In comes the lady with the alligator purse.
"Mumps," said the doctor,
"Measles," said the nurse,
"Nothing," said the lady with the alligator
purse.

The following jump rope rhymes were contributed by Janet Dubman's fourth grade class, Centinela School, Inglewood, California.

Cinderella thinks she's cute,
All she wears is a bathing suit.
If she counts to twenty-one,
You may have another turn.
1, 2, 3, ...

Jugs, Jugs,
Mama's gonna have a baby,
It ain't no boy,
It ain't no girl,
It's just an ordinary baby.
Wrap it up in tissue paper,
Throw it down the elevator.
First floor, STOP. (stop rope)
Second floor, STOP. (stop rope)
Third floor, STOP. (stop rope)
'Cause here comes the baby with the H-O-T.

Blue bells, cockle shells,
Eevie, ivy, over.
Mama's in the kitchen cookin' rice,
Daddy's outside, shootin' dice.
Baby's in the cradle, fast asleep,
And here come sister with the H-O-T.

Late last night or the night before,
Twenty-four robbers came a-knockin' at
    my door,
I let one in,
He hit me on the head with a rolling pin,
I ran outside,
The other one came in,
I got so scared, I went to bed.

SENIOR CITIZENS—ANCIENT CIVILIZATIONS

Ancient Egyptian	c. 3100–30 B.C.
Assyrian	c. 1100–600 B.C.
Aztec	1300s–1519 A.D.
Babylonian	c. 2000–1100 B.C.
Etruscan	800–500 B.C. (height of power)
Harappa (Indus Valley)	2500–1500 B.C.
Hittites	2000–1000 B.C.
Incan	1450–1532 A.D. (height of power)
Khmer civilization (Cambodia)	800–1200 A.D. (height of power)
Mayan	200–900 A.D. (height of power)
Minoan	1700–1400? B.D. (height of power)
Mycenaean	1400–1100 B.C. (height of power on mainland Greece)
Sumerian	c. 3200–2000 B.C.

Questions on Ancient Civilizations

1. Where was the civilization located?
2. What geographical features favored the development of the civilization?
3. How were the remains discovered or excavated?
4. What is known about the buildings?
5. What are some of the unanswered questions about the civilization?
6. What are some of the artifacts and works of art that remain? What do they tell about the people?
7. How was the civilization ruled?
8. What were some of the religious practices of the civilization?
9. What are some unique contributions or developments of the civilization?
10. What were the causes of the decline of the civilization?
11. What was the economy of the civilization based on?
12. Did the civilization have slaves? Where were they from? How were they treated?
13. List the civilizations in chronological order.

nine
ANIMALS

GOING, GOING, GONE
ENDANGERED AND EXTINCT ANIMALS

The endangered species on this list were obtained from the volumes of the *Red Data Book* compiled by the IUCN (International Union for the Conservation of Nature). Animals were selected to illustrate the various reasons for the decline of wildlife and the many kinds of species affected.

Going—classified as rare or vulnerable and likely to move into the endangered category in the near future if the reasons for their decline continue

Ceylon elephant found in eastern and southeastern Ceylon—killed by farmers whose lands are destroyed by migrating herds

Chimpanzee found in equatorial forests of Africa—captured for use in biomedical sciences as subjects for experiments, as pets, and for the animal trade; hunted for food and sport

Chinchilla found in Andes mountains of Chile and Bolivia—hunted and killed for its fur

Shortnose sturgeon, a small fish inhabiting Atlantic seaboard rivers—pollution of waters is a major factor as well as overfishing

Going–in danger of extinction; survival is not likely if the reasons for their decline continue

American crocodile found in Florida, Central America, parts of Mexico–killed for skins and sport; destruction of habitat, sometimes killed as a nuisance in docks

Arabian oryx found in Oman–they are declining because of uncontrolled hunting by organized hunting parties using cars and planes to overtake the animal

Beautiful parakeet found in Australia–main cause of extinction is excessive hunting and trapping for the aviculturist

Aye-Aye, forest-dwelling lemur of Madagascar–have suffered loss of habitat through forest clearance; killed by Malagasy people for superstitious reasons

Ciçek, a fish of Lake Egridir, Turkey–preyed upon by the pike-perch introduced in the lake in 1953, may already be extinct

Javan rhinoceros found in Indonesia–victims of overhunting for so-called medicinal products derived from their horns and blood

Orangutan, an ape inhabiting Borneo and Sumatra–destruction of forest habitat, captured for use by pet dealers, zoos, and research laboratories

Round Island boa found in Round Island (northwest of Mauritius)–goats and rabbits introduced to the island destroyed the ecological balance by eating the grasses leading to a reduction in the number of insects; insect-eating lizards used by the boa as food then diminished

San Francisco garter snake found in California–destruction of habitat due to housing development projects, control of waterflow, and removal of vegetation

South American river turtle (or arrau) found in tropical South America–hunted for eggs which are considered a delicacy, oil, meat, and the pet trade

Whooping crane, North America's tallest bird–victim of overhunting; loss of habitat due to drainage and fill of marshes

Gone–extinct

Arabian ostrich found in Saudi Arabia–hunted for sport in automobiles and airplanes

Catabasis acuminatus, a fish of the Rio Tieté, Brazil–pollution of headwaters of river by sewage from the city of São Paulo

Great auk found in Northern Europe and North America–killed for eggs, flesh, and feathered skin

Passenger pigeon found in eastern North America–trapped and shot for food and sport

Going, Going, Gone Activities

1. "Adopt" an endangered animal. Start a campaign to save it by writing pamphlets and slogans, making posters and bumper stickers.
2. On a world map, locate the country or countries where the endangered species are presently found. Make symbols to represent the animals' present status and place your symbols on the map.
3. Write fables or "Just So" stories to explain why an animal is endangered or extinct. Use factual information or make up your own. Here are some examples of titles: Bye-bye, Aye-aye; The Passing of the Passenger Pigeon; How the Chinchilla Lost Its Coat; The Cişek and the Pike-Perch.
4. Make a list of *other endangered and extinct things.* Endangered things might include buildings or historic sites in your city, the circus, hula hoops, and the door-to-door milkman; 23¢ a gallon for gas, the 5¢ cigar, Indian-head pennies, and the Pony Express could be on the extinct list.

ROCK-A-BYE BABY—NAMES FOR ANIMAL OFFSPRING

Animal	Offspring
bear	cub
beaver	kit
cat	kitten
chicken	chick
cow	calf
deer	fawn
dog	pup, puppy
eagle	eaglet
eel	elver
elephant	calf
fox	cub, kit
giraffe	calf
goat	kid
goose	gosling
hawk	eyas
horse	foal

Animal	Offspring
kangaroo	joey
lion	cub
otter	whelp
oyster	spat
pig	piglet, farrow, shoat
rabbit	bunny
rhinoceros	calf
seal	pup
sheep	lamb
swan	cygnet
tiger	cub
turkey	poult
whale	calf
wolf	cub, whelp

HERDS, SCHOOLS, AND FLOCKS—NAMES FOR ANIMAL GROUPS

Animal	Group Name
badgers	cete
bears	sloth
beavers	colony
bees	swarm
buffalo	gang
cats	clowder
chickens	flock
chicks	clutch
cows	herd
dogs	pack
ducks	brace, flock
elephants	herd
elks	gang
fish	school
foxes	skulk
geese	flock, gaggle (usually when grouped together on water)

Animal	Group Name
goats	flock
hawks	cast
hogs	drift
horses	herd
kangaroos	troop, mob
lions	pride
mallards	sord
monkeys	troop
partridges	covey
peacocks	muster
pheasants	nide
pigs	drove, litter
quails	bevy
rabbits	colony
seals	pod
sheep	drove, flock
turkeys	rafter
whales	gam, pod
wolves	pack, rout

6'S AND 8'S
PICTURESQUE NAMES OF INSECTS AND SPIDERS

ant lion
assassin bug
back swimmer
bald-faced hornet
bedbug
beefly
big green darner dragonfly
black widow spider
blister beetle
buffalo tree hopper
burying beetle
cabbage butterfly
carpenter ant
carpenter bee
carpet beetle
confused flower beetle
corn earworm
daddy longlegs (harvestman)
deathwatch beetle
dog-faced butterfly
earwig
engraver beetle
firefly
garden springtail
goliath beetle
greenbottle fly
gypsy moth
harlequin bug
June bug
lacewing
lady beetle (lady bug)
lightning bug
longhorn beetle
mayfly
monarch butterfly
paper wasp
praying mantis
punkies, no-see-ums (fly)
red admiral butterfly
robber fly
scorpion fly
silverfish
snowy tree cricket
soldier beetle
squashbug
squint-eye spider
sphinx moth
striped cucumber beetle
swallowtail butterfly
tarnished plant bug
tiger moth
tortoise beetle
trapdoor spider
triangle spider
turret spider
two-striped grasshopper
wanderer butterfly
water boatman
water penny beetle
water strider
whirligig beetle
wolf spider
yellow jacket
yellow woolybear (moth)
zebra spider

Activities With Insects and Spiders

1. Draw several of the insects and spiders as you think they would look, according to their names. Then compare your drawings with pictures of how the insects and spiders really look.
2. Categorize the insects and spiders into helpful and harmful groups.
3. Categorize the insects and spiders by their names, into groups such as colors, foods, animals, and jobs.

FAMOUS ANIMAL PEOPLE

Louis Agassiz–U.S. naturalist; famed for work on living and fossil forms of fish

J. J. Audubon–famous American naturalist and artist; one of the first to study and paint U.S. birds

Spencer F. Baird–naturalist and vertebrate zoologist

Rachel Carson–American marine biologist and science writer

Frank Chapman–American ornithologist; one of the first to study birds with the camera

Baron Cuvier–French naturalist; first to compare the structure of animal bodies with that of man

Charles Darwin–British naturalist; developed theory of evolution based on natural selection that revolutionized the biological sciences

Raymond Lee Ditmars–noted American authority on reptiles; wrote many popular reptile books; developed a snakebite serum

William Henry Hudson–English author and naturalist; wrote articles and books on nature, particularly bird life

Sir Julian Huxley–noted British biologist

Thomas Huxley–famous zoologist, lecturer, and writer

Carolus Linnaeus–developed a scientific classification system of animals and plants

Clinton Hart Merriam–American physician and zoologist; helped found the National Geographic Society in 1888

Jan Swammerdam–Dutch anatomist and zoologist; pioneered in the anatomy of insects; his work formed the basis of entomology

Nicolaas Tinbergen–Dutch-born zoologist; studies how behavior of animals adapts to the environment

Jane Goodall Van Lawick–English zoologist; became famous for behavior studies of chimpanzees

Alexander Wilson–one of the founders of American ornithology

ANIMALOGISTS

biologist—scientist who studies living organisms

biosociologist—an ecologist who studies environments of groups of living things, such as schools of fish

conchologist—zoologist who studies mollusks or shells

ecologist—biologist who studies the relationship between organisms and their environment

embryologist—biologist who studies the formation and development of living things prior to birth

entomologist—zoologist who specializes in the study of insects

helminthologist—zoologist who studies worms

herpetologist—zoologist who studies reptiles and amphibians

ichthyologist—zoologist who specializes in the study of fishes

limnologist—biologist who studies the biological, chemical, geographical, and physical features of lakes and ponds (fresh waters)

malacologist—zoologist who studies mollusks

mammalogist—zoologist who specializes in the study of mammals

morphologist—biologist who examines animal form and structure

ornithologist—zoologist who specializes in the study of birds

physiologist—biologist who studies the normal functions of living things

taxonomist—scientist who names and classifies animals

zoographer—an ecologist who studies the distribution of animals in the various regions of the world

zoologist—scientist who studies animals and their classification

AWARDS TO ANIMALS

Selecting an animal to study can be more fun if you know some interesting animal facts. Here are some animals who have earned awards for outstanding achievement. These awards can be displayed in an *awards gallery* from which children choose an animal to study.

Maxi Awards

blue whale—largest and heaviest mammal
African elephant—largest land animal
giraffe—tallest animal
Kodiak bear—largest land carnivore
Siberian tiger—largest member of the cat family
springboks—largest herds
gorilla—largest primate
mandrill—largest member of the monkey family
Irish wolfhound—tallest breed of dog
ostrich—largest bird, with the largest eye of any land animal
giant squid—largest eye of any living or extinct animal, land or sea
wandering albatross—bird with the largest wing span
bald eagle—builds the largest nests
crocodile—largest reptile
Komodo monitor—largest lizard
anaconda—longest and heaviest of all snakes
Chinese giant salamander—largest amphibian
goliath frog—largest frog
marine toad—largest toad
whale shark—largest fish
white shark—largest carnivorous fish
nephila spider—has the largest spider web
goliath beetle—heaviest insect
stick-insect—longest insect
giant birdwing—largest butterfly*

*Most probable.

Mini Awards

pygmy shrew—smallest mammal
sea otter—smallest totally marine mammal
bee hummingbird—smallest bird
gecko—smallest reptile*
thread snake—shortest snake*
dwarf pygmy goby—shortest fish*
common housefly—shortest-lived insect*
dwarf blue butterfly—smallest butterfly*

*Most probable.

From *The Guinness Book of Animal Facts and Feats,* Gerald L. Wood (Guinness Superlatives Ltd., Great Britain, 1972)

Tortoise and Hare Awards

pronghorn antelope—fastest land animal over a sustained distance

cheetah—fastest land animal over a short distance

three-toed sloth—slowest moving land mammal

spine-tailed swift—fastest flying bird

black mamba—fastest moving land snake*

dragonfly—fastest flying insect

marlin—fastest fish over a sustained distance

sea horse—slowest moving marine fish

Senior Citizens Award

killer whale—longest-lived mammal (except man)

Asiatic elephant—longest-lived land mammal (except man)

queen termite—longest-lived insect

Whiz Kids Award

chimpanzee—most intelligent primate (except man)

baboon—most intelligent member of the monkey family

Bad Guy Awards

king cobra—longest venomous snake

diamondback rattler—heaviest venomous snake

Kokoi arrow poison frog—most poisonous animal ever recorded

stonefish—most venomous sting

Japanese puffer fish—most poisonous fish if eaten

piranha—most ferocious fish

black widow—most venomous spider

blue-ringed octopus—most dangerous octopus

Maternity Award

Asiatic elephant—longest mammal gestation period

The Big Sleep Award

edible dormouse—mammal longest in hibernation

The Now Hear This Award

bat—most highly developed sense of hearing (among mammals)

Thick Skin Award

whale shark—the thickest skin of any animal

Broad Jump Award

red kangaroo—longest recorded leap

Loud Mouth Award

male cicada—loudest insect

Bon Voyage Award

Arctic tern—longest migration of flying birds

Architect's Award

termites—master builders of the world

*Most probable.

Beastly Questions

1. Why could the ziczac be called "the crocodile's best friend"?
2. Where would you find some pinnipeds?
3. Which animal would get the Most Unusual Animal Award? Why?
4. Why do some animals estivate?
5. Why are some people called "dodos"?
6. What do the aardvark and the anteater have in common?
7. What is the bear's "Keep-Out" sign?
8. In the old days, why did women who wore corsets need whales?
9. How does a zoo rhino or elephant get a pedicure?
10. How does the platypus break all the rules of nature?
11. Why can't ants be called "litterbugs"?
12. How does the cave fish manage without any eyes?
13. How would you prepare for a hermit crab houseguest?
14. What five features makes the camel well adapted for desert travel?
15. What do the cows, horses, and dogs of the ocean look like?
16. How do you feed a giraffe?
17. What are some special jobs dogs are trained to do?
18. What are an *Adobenus rosmarus* and a *Thalarctos maritimus*?
19. What would you find in a Tiergarten?
20. What is a pangolin?
21. How is a jerboa like a kangaroo?
22. Which animals ruminate?
23. How do birds sing?
24. How does a raccoon carry its babies?
25. How does a flying squirrel fly?
26. Why don't spiders get caught in their own webs?
27. What does the S.P.C.A. do for animals?
28. How does a bat "see with its ears"?
29. What's odd about the way sloths live?
30. What is the layout of a prairie dog's home?
31. Where does a snake's tail begin?
32. What does a lepidopterist collect?
33. What happens when insects stridulate?
34. Why can a fly walk on the ceiling?
35. How are an octopus and a squid like a jet?

THE ____________ AWARD

IS PRESENTED TO ______________________

animal's name

FOR ______________________

(animal's outstanding characteristic)

Description of Animal: ______________________

Habitat: ______________________

Interesting Facts: ______________________

____

____

____

Draw a picture of the animal in its natural habitat and paste in here.

Name:

Date:

DINOSAURS

ALLOSAURUS meat eater

more than thirty feet long

moved on two large hind legs, used powerful tail for support in walking or standing

ANATOSAURUS plant eater

about forty feet long

walked on two legs, used tail for support; had as many as 2,000 teeth

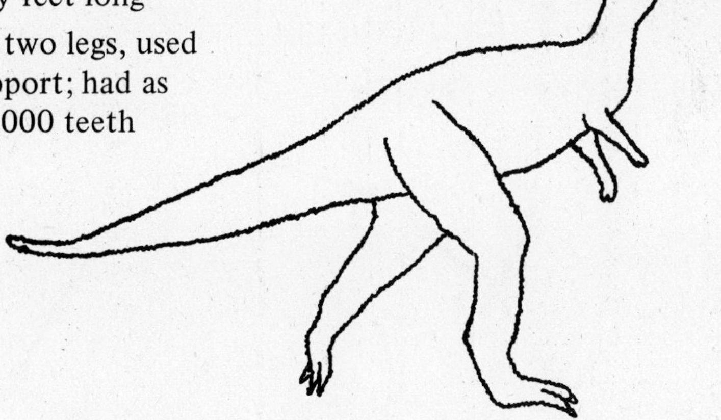

ANKYLOSAURUS plant eater

about ten feet long

body was covered with overlapping bony plates with a row of spikes along each side; clublike tail tipped with a heavy mass of bone

BRACHIOSAURUS plant eater

seventy feet long, weighed eighty-four short tons

largest of all the dinosaurs

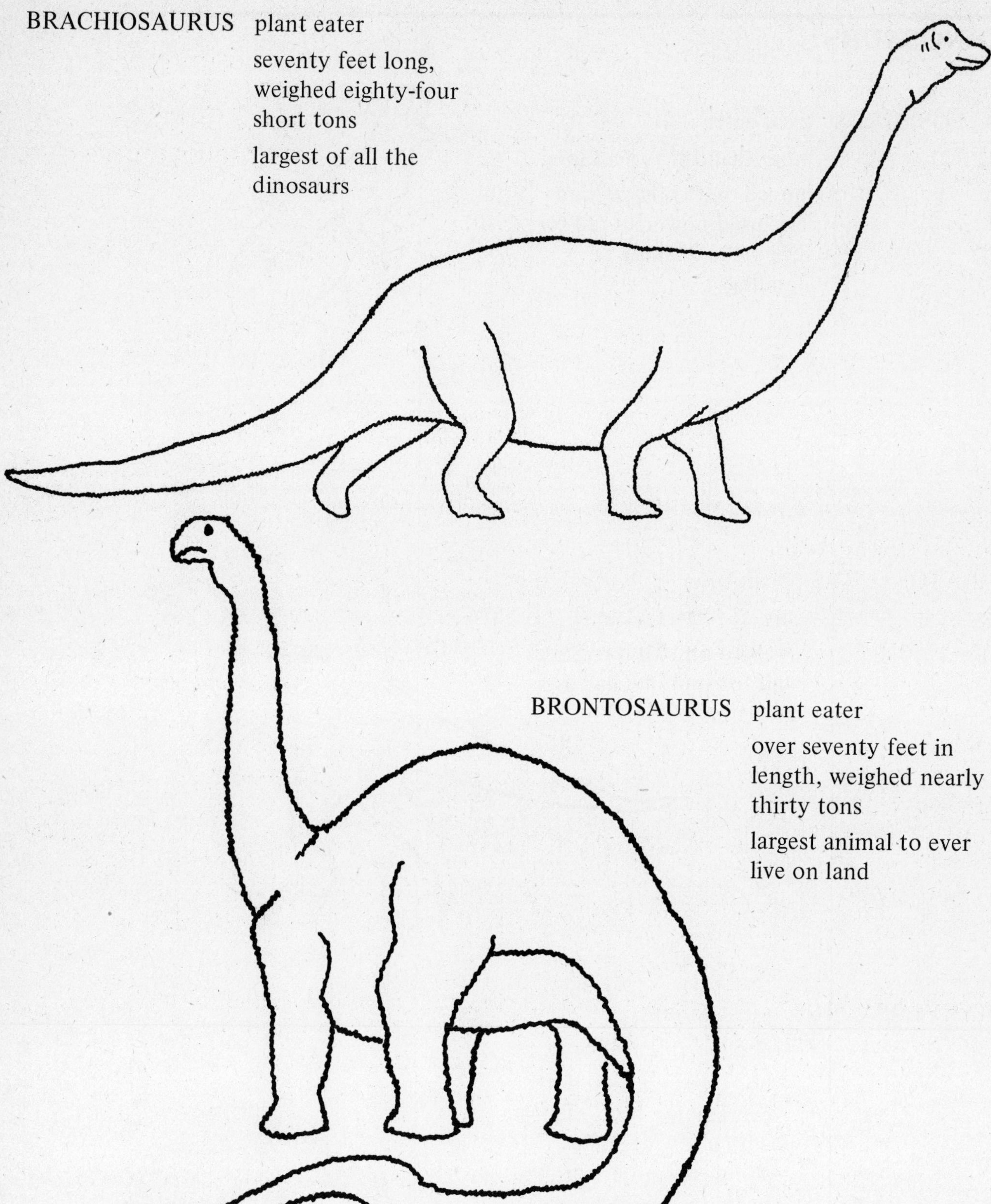

BRONTOSAURUS plant eater

over seventy feet in length, weighed nearly thirty tons

largest animal to ever live on land

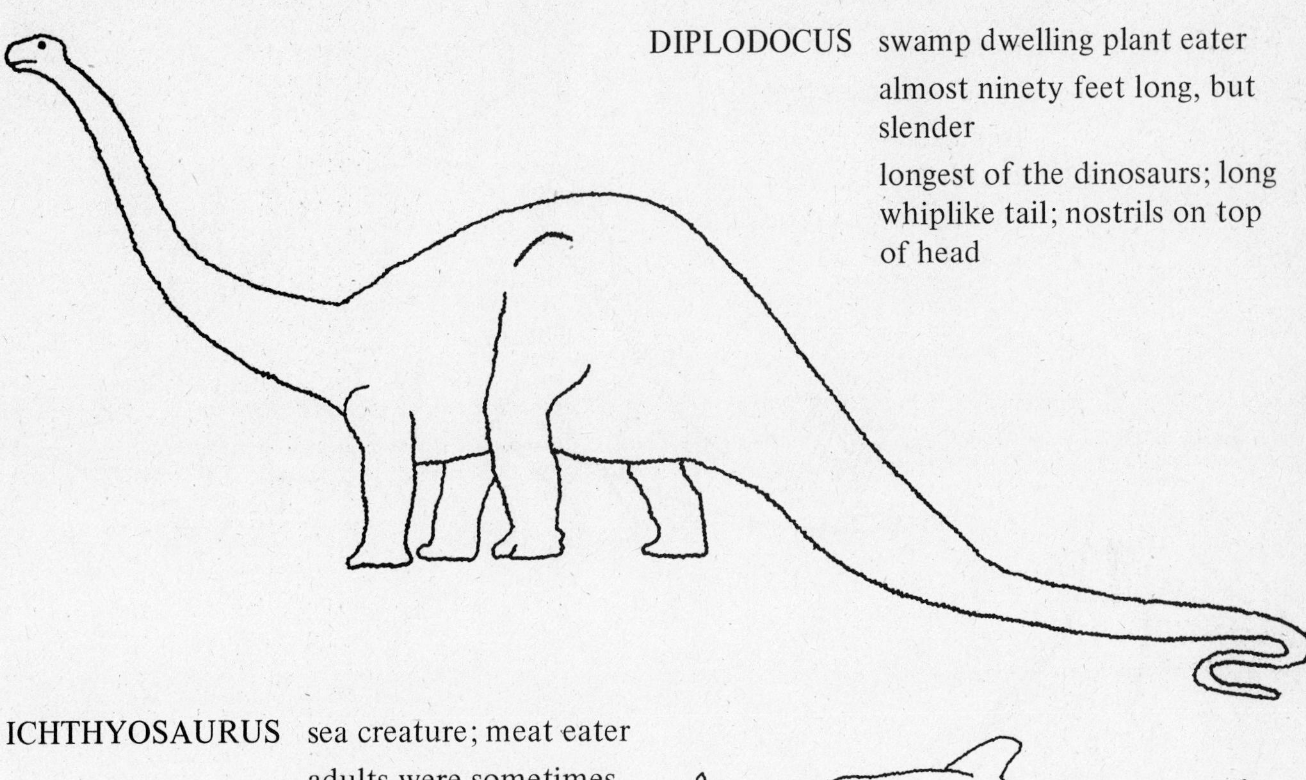

DIPLODOCUS
swamp dwelling plant eater

almost ninety feet long, but slender

longest of the dinosaurs; long whiplike tail; nostrils on top of head

ICHTHYOSAURUS
sea creature; meat eater

adults were sometimes forty feet long

body shape similar to sharks; mouth filled with teeth needed for catching and holding fish

MEGALOSAURUS
meat eater

stood almost twelve feet high

walked on hind legs; large head with sharp teeth; small front legs

PTERANODON
meat eater, ate fish and small flying things

wingspread of nearly thirty feet; small stumpy body that probably weighed no more than twenty-five or thirty pounds

largest of the flying reptiles (pterodactyl or pterosaurus); had no teeth or tail; long skull with a protruding bony crest

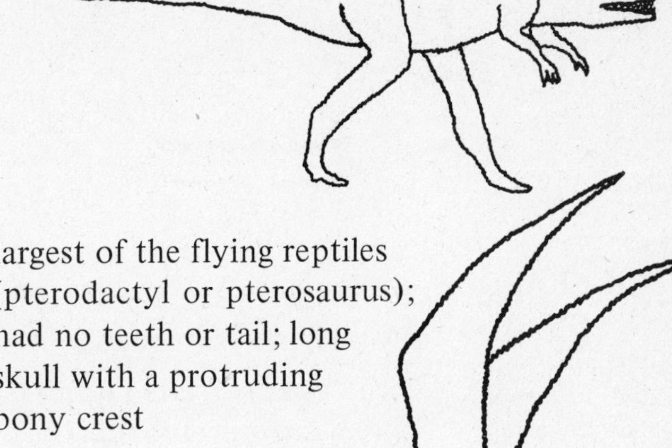

STEGOSAURUS plant eater

about eighteen feet long

triangular bony plates protected its neck, back, and tail; brain about the size of a walnut

TRACHODON plant eater

thirty to forty feet long

duck-billed; walked on hind legs

TRICERATOPS plant eater

twenty-five feet long

bony armor covered head; three horns protruded from head

TYRANNOSAURUS REX largest meat eater

measured fifty feet from nose to tail, stood about twenty feet high

had six-inch razor-sharp teeth

Dinosaur Activities

1. Make a graph of the lengths of the dinosaurs.
2. Categorize the dinosaurs into two groups, carnivores and herbivores.
3. Convert the lengths of the dinosaurs into meters.
4. Use the length of a car, bed, or other large thing as a unit of measure. Convert the lengths of the dinosaurs into this unit. For example, ankylosaurus = about one car
5. Choose a dinosaur and a familiar melody. Make up lyrics to fit the melody, using the information on the dinosaur list. Here's a song about a trachodon to be sung to the melody of Three Blind Mice.

   Trachodon, Trachodon,
   Duck-billed mouth, duck-billed mouth,
   He walked about on his two hind legs,
   His length was thirty to forty feet,
   Did you ever see such a sight in your life as
   Trachodon.

PART 4

THE ARTS

ten
ART AND MUSIC

HUES, BLUES, AND FUGUES
ART AND MUSIC CATEGORIES

Here's a list of art and music pieces grouped within some interesting categories. One way to use this list is to integrate a category with a usual topic of study. For example, Wind, Rain, Sleet, and Snow can be combined with a study of weather or the seasons. Another way is to begin with a category and expand into other subject areas and skills. For example, art and music activities that take place as a result of exposure to works in the category, Beauty in the Beast, can lead to other experiences. These experiences might include writing original stories and poems, reading animal tales, and making scientific reports and observations.

Art

SHOW BIZ

Le Cirque–Georges Seurat

La Parade (The Side Show)–Georges Seurat

Broadway Boogie Woogie–Piet Mondrian

Three Musicians–Pablo Picasso

Three Dancers–Pablo Picasso

Clown–Henri de Toulouse-Lautrec

Cafe Concert at Les Ambassadeurs–Edgar Degas

Rehearsal in the Foyer of the Opera–Edgar Degas

Music

SHOW BIZ

Circus Polka–Igor Stravinsky

"The Shrovetide Fair" from Petrouchka Ballet Suite–Igor Stravinsky

"Vesti La Giubba" from Pagliacci–Ruggiero Leoncavallo

"Clowns" from A Midsummer Night's Dream–Felix Mendelssohn

"Circus Music" from The Red Pony–Aaron Copland

Art

COLORS

Composition in Red, Blue, and Yellow—Piet Mondrian

Harmony in Red—Henri Matisse

Park Near L(ucerne)—Paul Klee

The Red Studio—Henri Matisse

Cow's Skull—Red, White, and Blue—Georgia O'Keeffe

ON THE ROAD

End of the Trail—James Earle Fraser

In the Catskills—Thomas Cole

View of Toledo—El Greco (Domenicos Theotocopoulos)

The Scout: Friends or Enemies? —Frederick Remington

Boulevard Montmartre, Paris —Camille Pissarro

ALL IN THE FAMILY

The Family—Marisol

Arrangement in Black and Grey: The Artist's Mother—James McNeill Whistler

An Old Man and His Grandson —Domenico Ghirlandaio

The Peale Family—Charles Willson Peale

Mother and Child with Bird —Suzuki Harunobu

American Gothic—Grant Wood

The Mother and Sister of the Artist —Berthe Morisot

A Father's Curse: The Ungrateful Son —Jean Baptiste Greuze

Family Promenade—Paul Klee

Music

COLORS

Rhapsody in Blue—George Gershwin

Fantasia on "Greensleeves"—English folk song, composer unknown—adapted and orchestrated by Ralph Vaughn Williams

Mood Indigo—Duke Ellington

Le Train bleu—Darius Milhaud

Ebony Concerto—Igor Stravinsky

ON THE ROAD

An American in Paris—George Gershwin

Grand Canyon Suite—Ferde Grofé

The Little Train of Caipira —Heitor Villa-Lobos

St. Louis Blues—W. C. Handy

Cockaigne (In London Town) —Sir Edward Elgar

In the Steppes of Central Asia —Alexander Borodin

ALL IN THE FAMILY

The Cradle Song—Johannes Brahms

"Brother Come and Dance with Me" from Hansel and Gretel—Engelbert Humperdinck

The Nursery—Modest Moussorgsky

The Bartered Bride—Bedřich Smetana

"The Bridal Procession" from Lohengrin —Richard Wagner

Prole do Bébé (Baby's Family) —Heitor Villa-Lobos

"Curious Story" from Kinderscenen —Robert Schumann

Art

A.M. AND P.M.

The Starry Night–Vincent Van Gogh

An Impression: Sunrise–Claude Monet

Nighthawks–Edward Hopper

Day and Night–M. C. Escher

WHAT'S MY LINE?

The Gleaners–Jean François Millet

The Sower–Jean François Millet

The Lacemaker–Jan Vermeer

Washerwomen–Honoré Daumier

The Stone Breakers–Gustave Courbet

Sugar Cane–Diego Rivera

Wagon Boss–Charles Russell

The Anatomy Lesson–Rembrandt van Rijn

Jockeys in the Rain–Edgar Degas

The Boxers–Alexander Archipenko

H_2O

Hollow of the Deep-Sea Wave –Katsushika Hokusai

Water Lillies–Claude Monet

The Boating Party–Mary Cassatt

Breezing Up–Winslow Homer

Fur Traders on the Missouri–George Caleb Bingham

Wave, Night–Georgia O'Keeffe

Music

A.M. AND P.M.

Vincent (Starry, Starry Night)–Don McLean

Moonlight Sonata–Ludwig van Beethoven

Morning Mood from "Peer Gynt" –Edvard Grieg

Nights in the Gardens of Spain –Manuel de Falla

Stardust–Hoagy Carmichael

WHAT'S MY LINE?

The Barber of Seville–Gioacchino Rossini

Sorcerer's Apprentice–Paul Dukas

Rodeo–Aaron Copland

Spinning Song–Franz Schubert

Spinning Song, Op. 67, No. 4–Felix Mendelssohn

"Where Are the Clowns?" from A Little Night Music–Stephen Sondheim

H.M.S. Pinafore–Gilbert and Sullivan

Zar und Zimmermann (The Czar and the Carpenter)–Albert Lortzing

The Harmonius Blacksmith–George Frederick Handel

H_2O

La Mer–Claude Debussy

"Barcarolle" from The Tales of Hoffmann –Jacques Offenbach

Venetian Boat Song–Felix Mendelssohn

Die Moldau–Bedřich Smetana

On the Beautiful Blue Danube–Johann Strauss

"The Rhine Motive" from Das Rheingeld –Richard Wagner

Water Music–George Frederick Handel

Art

THE ARTS IN ART

High Kick—Edgar Degas

The Yellow Violin—Raoul Dufy

Musical Forms—Georges Braque

The Artist in His Studio—Jan Vermeer

Claude Monet in His Floating Studio —Èdouard Manet

MOTHER NATURE

Flowering Trees—Piet Mondrian

Blue Landscape—Paul Cézanne

Hampstead Heath—John Constable

May Day—Andrew Wyeth

Photographs by Eliot Porter and Ansel Adams

DREAMS AND FANTASY

The Dream—Henri Rousseau

Sweet Dreams—Paul Gauguin

The Harlequin's Carnival—Joan Miró

Casa Milá Apartment House, Barcelona —Antoni Gaudí

Church of Notre-Dame-du-Haut —Le Corbusier

I and the Village—Marc Chagall

Music

THE ARTS IN ART

Pictures from an Exhibition—Modest Moussorgsky

Matthias the Painter—Paul Hindemith

Walt Whitman—Dmitri Shostakovich

Seven Studies on Themes of Paul Klee —Gunther Schuller

"The Poet Speaks" from Kinderscenen —Robert Schumann

MOTHER NATURE

Tales from the Vienna Woods —Johann Strauss

Symphony No. 6 (The Pastoral) —Ludwig van Beethoven

Out of Doors Suite—Béla Bártok

Spring Symphony—Robert Schumann

Italian Symphony—Felix Mendelssohn

My Country—Bedřich Smetana

"Waltz of the Flowers" from the Nutcracker Suite—Peter Ilyich Tchaikovsky

DREAMS AND FANTASY

Mother Goose Suite—Maurice Ravel

Hansel and Gretel—Engelbert Humperdinck

The Nutcracker Suite—Peter Ilyich Tchaikovsky

Incidental Music to A Midsummer Night's Dream—Felix Mendelssohn

Scheherazade—Nicholas Rimsky-Korsakoff

"The Fantasy Overture" from Romeo and Juliet—Peter Ilyich Tchaikovsky

Firebird Suite—Igor Stravinsky

Art

NIGHTMARES

The Nightmare–John Henry Fuseli

The Dream–Max Beckmann

The Persistence of Memory–Salvador Dali

House of Stairs–M. C. Escher

The Garden of Delights–Hieronymus Bosch

The Storm–Yves Tanguy

The Scream–Edvard Munch

Demon as Pirate–Paul Klee

Swamp Angel–Max Ernst

BEAUTY IN THE BEAST

Two Bison–Lascaux cave painting

Crane–Katsushika Hokusai

Fantastic Rhinoceros–Albrecht Dürer

The Hare–Albrecht Dürer

Exotic Landscape–Henri Rousseau

Tiger in the Rain–Henri Rousseau

Peaceable Kingdom–Edward Hicks

Wild Turkey–J. J. Audubon

Bird in Space (sculpture) –Constantin Brancusi

Lobster Trap and Fish Tail (mobile) –Alexander Calder

Dog–Alberto Giacometti

THREE'S A CROWD

Peasant Dance–Pieter Bruegel

People Waiting–Honoré Daumier

The Night Watch–Rembrandt van Rijn

The School of Athens–Raphael

Visit of the Magi–Benozzo Gozzoli

Music

NIGHTMARES

Danse Macabre–Camille Saint-Saëns

Night on Bald Mountain–Modest Moussorgsky

Baba Yaga–Anatol Ĺiadov

El Amor Brujo–Manuel de Falla

BEAUTY IN THE BEAST

Papillon No. 8–Robert Schumann

Papillon–Edvard Grieg

Flight of the Bumblebee–Nicholas Rimsky-Korsakoff

The Nightingale–Dmitri Shostakovich

The Swan Lake Ballet–Peter Ilyich Tchaikovsky

Afternoon of a Faun–Claude Debussy

Peter and the Wolf–Sergei Prokofiev

Carnival of the Animals–Camille Saint-Saëns

Bear Dance–Béla Bártok

THREE'S A CROWD

"Pilgrim's Chorus" from Tannhäuser –Richard Wagner

"Hallelujah Chorus" from Messiah –George Frederick Handel

Symphony No. 8, in Eb major (Symphony of a Thousand)–Gustav Mahler

Art

GIVE ME YOUR TIRED, YOUR POOR . . .

The Third Class Carriage–Honoré Daumier

The Potato-Eaters–Vincent Van Gogh

Victims (detail from University of Guadalajara Mural Cycle)–José Clemente Orozco

Peasants Carrying Brushwood–Jean François Millet

The Liberation of the Peon–Diego Rivera

Breadline–Reginald Marsh

FUN AND GAMES

A Sunday Afternoon on the Grand Jatte –Georges Seurat

Swimmers–Katsushika Hokusai

Children's Games–Pieter Bruegel

Le Moulin de la Galette–Auguste Renoir

Bathers–Georges Seurat

The Card Players–Paul Cézanne

Boating–Èdouard Manet

Jockeys Before the Grandstand –Edgar Degas

WINING AND DINING

Campbell's Soup–Andy Warhol

The Basket of Apples–Paul Cézanne

Still Life–Diego Velázquez

Pie–Roy Lichtenstein

The Diner–George Segal

Giant Hamburger (sculpture) –Claes Oldenburg

Music

GIVE ME YOUR TIRED, YOUR POOR . . .

Porgy and Bess–George Gershwin

Peasant Cantata–Johann Sebastian Bach

La Bohème–Giacomo Puccíni

Poet and Peasant Overture–Franz von Suppé

The Threepenny Opera–Kurt Weill, Bertholt Brecht

The Cradle Will Rock–Marc Blitzstein

Scenes from Peasant Life–Edvard Grieg

FUN AND GAMES

"The Toreador Song" from Carmen –Georges Bizet

Children's Games–Georges Bizet

Toy Symphony–Joseph Haydn

Till Eulenspiegel's Merry Pranks –Richard Strauss

Roman Carnival Overture–Louis Hector Berlioz

Camptown Races–Stephen Foster

WINING AND DINING

The Love for Three Oranges–Sergei Prokofiev

"Breakfast Waltz, Waiter's Waltz, Dinner Music" from Der Rosenkavalier –Richard Strauss

Yorkshire Feast Song–Henry Purcell

"The Drinking Song" from La Traviata –Giuseppe Verdi

Whipped Cream (ballet)–Richard Strauss

The Long Christmas Dinner–Paul Hindemith

Art

A HOUSE IS NOT A HOME

Taj Mahal, India

Mosque of Ahmed I, Istanbul

Notre-Dame, Paris

Pyramids, Egypt

Robie House, Chicago–Frank Lloyd Wright

Lake Shore Drive Apartment Houses –Mies Van der Rohe

Monticello–Thomas Jefferson

Parthenon, Athens

Kinkakuji (the Golden Pavilion), Kyoto

WIND, RAIN, SLEET, AND SNOW

Primavera–Sandro Botticelli

The Return of the Hunters–Pieter Bruegel

The Old Checkered House–Grandma Moses (Anna Mary Robertson Moses)

Waterloo Bridge (Effects of Mist) –Claude Monet

Landscapes of the Four Seasons –Tsunenobu

Threatening Weather–Rene Magritte

NUTS AND BOLTS

Computer Landscape–David Pease

Twittering Machine–Paul Klee

Brooklyn Bridge–Joseph Stella

Music

A HOUSE IS NOT A HOME

Skyscrapers (ballet)–John Alden Carpenter

My Old Kentucky Home–Stephen Foster

We Are Building a City (children's opera) –Paul Hindemith

Quiet City–Aaron Copland

WIND, RAIN, SLEET, AND SNOW

The Four Seasons–Antonio Vivaldi

Clouds, Mists–Claude Debussy

The Rite of Spring–Igor Stravinsky

"The Snow Is Dancing" from Children's Corner Suite–Claude Debussy

"The Storm and the Calm" from William Tell Overture–Gioacchino Rossini

Appalachian Spring–Aaron Copland

Summer Music for Woodwind Quartet –Samuel Barber

"A Masque of the Seasons" from The Fairy Queen–Henry Purcell

Raindrop Prelude–Frédéric Chopin

NUTS AND BOLTS

The Telephone–Gian-Carlo Menotti

Dance of Steel–Sergei Prokofiev

Catalogue of Agricultural Implements –Darius Milhaud

Pacific 231–Arthur Honneger

Art

WAR AND PEACE

Guernica–Pablo Picasso

The Executions of the 3rd of May –Francisco de Goya

Battle of the Amazons –Peter Paul Rubens

St. George–Donatello (sculpture)

Mona Lisa–Leonardo da Vinci

Recumbent Figure–Henry Moore (sculpture)

Peace–Jacques Lipchitz (sculpture)

The Kiss–Auguste Rodin (sculpture)

The Kiss–Constantin Brancusi (sculpture)

Love–Robert Indiana (sculpture)

THIS IS ME

SELF-PORTRAITS

Leonardo da Vinci

Peter Paul Rubens

Rembrandt van Rijn

Henri Rousseau

Joan Miró

Amedeo Modigliani

Vincent Van Gogh

Francisco de Goya

Hieronymus Bosch

HIDDEN PICTURES

The Adoration of the Magi –Sandro Botticelli

The Maids of Honor–Diego Velazquez

The Last Judgment–Michaelangelo

At the Moulin Rouge–Henri de Toulouse-Lautrec

The Artist's Studio–Gustave Courbet

Music

WAR AND PEACE

March Militaire–Franz Schubert

Liebestraum–Franz Liszt

The Story of a Soldier–Igor Stravinsky

Light Cavalry Overture–von Suppe

1812 Overture–Peter Ilyich Tchaikovsky

Peace Train–Cat Stevens

Wellington's Victory or the Battle of Vittoria–Ludwig van Beethoven

Peace–Cándido Portinari

THIS IS ME

SELF-PORTRAITS

From My Life–Bedřich Smetana

From Memories of Childhood –Modest Moussorgsky

ART PERIODS AND STYLES

The following brief descriptions contain some of the significant characteristics of an art period or style. Although art experts sometimes disagree on exact dates and artists of a period or style, approximate dates and representative works that are generally agreed upon are listed.

Gothic (c. 1150 - 1500)

Originated in France in the mid 1100s and spread to England, Germany, Italy, and other parts of Europe during the 1200s; great heights, lightness, and grace characterized Gothic architecture; pointed arches and tall, slender columns rose to cross-ribbed vaulting supported by flying buttresses, and stained glass windows depicted religious stories. During this period many painters worked as illuminators, illustrating and decorating expensive manuscript copies of the Gospels and prayer books; compositions became richer and more complex; people were given distinguishing features and personalities, and greater attention was paid to detail of plants, trees, and flowers—species became recognizable; introduction of the third dimension as painters attempted to depict depth; other forms of Gothic art include stone carvings, iron screens, metalwork using filigree, enamels and precious stones, and tapestries.

Rheims Cathedral—France
Notre-Dame Cathedral—France
Chartres Cathedral—France
Westminster Abbey—England
Milan Cathedral—Italy
Giotto—Madonna Enthroned
Gentile da Fabriano—The Adoration of the Magi
Master Honoré—Prayer Book of Phillip the Fair

Renaissance (c. 1400 - 1600)

A characteristic of Renaissance art was the development of linear perspective in pictures, use of lights and shadows to create depth, and graceful figures with more attention paid to anatomy and realism.

Donatello—David
Fra Angelico—The Annunciation
Sandro Botticelli—The Birth of Venus
Titian—Bacchanal
Leonardo da Vinci—Mona Lisa
Raphael—School of Athens
Michelangelo—Moses
Jan van Eyck—The Arnolfini Wedding
Pieter Bruegel—Peasant Wedding
Albrecht Dürer—Knight, Death, and Devil

Mannerism (c. 1520 - 1600)

A term that defines the transitional period from the high Renaissance to Baroque; the art often portrayed a historic event as a contemporary happening; paintings were characterized by exaggerated poses and elongation of the human figure, strange perspective, and unsteady light.

Parmigianino—The Madonna with the Long Neck
Tintoretto—The Last Supper
El Greco—The Burial of Count Orgaz

Baroque (c. 1600 - 1750)

Baroque art and architecture is characterized by flowing movement, swelling forms, grandiose dimensions, great activity, and dramatic detail. Architecture, sculpture, and painting were frequently combined into an integral work of art; architects combined Classical and Renaissance elements such as columns, arches, and capitals; sweeping curves replaced rectangular areas; greater emphasis was placed on city planning and landscape design; artists used techniques such as foreshortening and asymmetrical designs; drama was heightened by the theatrical use of lighting.

Gian Lorenzo Bernini—Fountain of the Four Rivers, Piazza Navona, Rome
Francesco Borromini—S. Carl alle Quartro Fontane
Dominikus Zimmermann—Die Wies, Bavaria, Germany
Annibale Carracci—Farnese Gallery ceiling
Michelangelo Caravaggio—Calling of St. Matthew
Peter Paul Rubens—The Garden of Love
Diego Velazquez—The Maids of Honor
Frans Hals—Yonker Ramp and His Sweetheart
Rembrandt—Night Watch

Rococo (c. 1720 - 1780)

Style developed out of Baroque; art communicated a feeling of relaxation and gaiety as opposed to the serious, heroic style of Baroque; paintings characterized by bright, shimmering surfaces and poetic, light-hearted imaginary themes.

Jean Honoré Fragonard—The Swing
Antoine Watteau—Mezzetin

Neoclassicism (c. 1750 - 1850)

Evolved as a reaction against Baroque and Rococo; art and architecture is marked by simplicity of design and restraint in the use of ornamentation; paintings characterized by strong contrasts of color, firmly modeled forms, balance and order.

Jean Auguste Dominique Ingres–Odalisque
Jacques Louis David–Napoleon Crossing the Alps

Romanticism (c. 1800 - 1840)

Paintings expressed the emotion and imagination of the artists; emotional and symbolic qualities of a myth often combined with the representation of an ordinary event or scene to create a feeling of mystery; paintings characterized by vigorous brush strokes, vibrant color and deep shadows.

Theodore Gericault–Mounted Officer of the Imperial Guard
Eugène Delacroix–Greece on the Ruins of Missolonghi
Honoré Daumier–The Third Class Carriage
Joseph M. W. Turner–The Slave Ship

Realism (c. 1848 - 1900)

Differed from Romanticism in its insistence upon fact without idealization, on the real rather than the imaginary or ideal, on the present rather than the past; paintings were based on the artist's unsentimental view of life around him; many European and American artists continue to paint in this style today.

Gustave Courbet–The Stone Breakers

Impressionism (c. 1870 - 1910)

Like the Realists, the Impressionists painted scenes of everyday life, but their painting style was based on the continual changes of nature–light transforming objects, reflections altering color and form. Painters reproduced the effect or "impression" of things at a particular moment in time, recorded what they saw rather than what they knew about an object. Favorite subjects included scenes from the world of entertainment–cafés, concerts, the theater; pictures characterized by gaiety, sparkle, shimmering, luminous colors, freshness of color, free brushwork.

Claude Monet–The Cathedral at Rouen
Edgar Degas–Woman with Chrysanthemums
Pierre Auguste Renoir–Lunch of the Boating Party at Bougival
Mary Cassatt–The Bath
Camille Pissarro–Afternoon at the Boulevard des Italiens

Post Impressionism (c. 1886 - 1905)

Post Impressionists label a group of artists who had at first accepted Impressionism, but went beyond it in various directions; artists of this period were not bound by a common goal or style, but pursued individual styles.

Georges Seurat–La Baignade
Vincent van Gogh–Sunflowers
Paul Cézanne–Mont Sainte Victoire
Paul Gauguin–La Orana Maria

Expressionism (early 1900s)

Interpreted reality in a highly personal manner; paintings are often characterized by distortion and exaggeration of color and form.

Henri de Toulouse-Lautrec–Dance at the Moulin Rouge
Henri Rousseau–The Sleeping Gypsy

Fauvism (c. 1903 - 1907)

Labeled the *fauves* (wild beasts) when they shocked the public with paintings filled with brilliant colors, bold distortions, and simple designs; influenced and encouraged by non-European cultures to seek new ways to communicate emotions; paintings characterized by rich surface texture, lively pattern, discordant color combinations, and sweeping brushstrokes; expression of emotion was more important than objective representation; continued the trends begun by Van Gogh and Gauguin.

Henri Matisse–The Joy of Life
Georges Rouault–The Old King
Chaim Soutine–The Dead Fowl

Die Brucke (c. 1904 - 1913)

The name means the Bridge. Members of this German society produced paintings especially expressive of intense human feelings; used vigorous brushwork, bold lines, strong colors, and distorted contours.

Max Beckmann–The Dream
Emil Nolde–Masks and Dahlias
Oskar Kokoschka–Tempest

Der Blaue Reiter (c. 1909 - 1913)

The name means the Blue Rider, title of a Kandinsky picture. Group of Munich artists led by Wassily Kandinsky who totally discarded representation. By using bright colors and free brushwork he created a completely nonobjective style.

Wassily Kandinsky—Accompanied Contrast
Paul Klee—Fish Magic
Franz Marc—The Fate of Animals

Cubism (c. 1907 - 1914)

Subject matter broken up into a series of flat planes and basic geometric shapes and arranged in complex interlocking and overlapping relationships; multiple sides of an object were shown at the same time.

Juan Gris—La Table du Café, Abstraction in Gray
Pablo Picasso—Ambroise Vollard
Georges Braque—The Musician's Table
Fernand Léger—The City
Jacques Lipchitz—Man with Mandolin

Orphism

Developed by Robert Delaunay, it retained geometric patterns of Cubism, but used brighter colors and avoided the depiction of recognizable subject matter, as in Delaunay's *Circular Forms.*

Dadaism (c. 1916 - 1922)

Dada emerged as a protest against the violence and destruction of World War I; broke all the rules and traditions of art and society; nonsense, absurdity, and antiart prevailed in the works of the Dadaists; opened the way for invention and creativity; art no longer was dependent on manual craftsmanship or established rules.

Marcel Duchamp—To be looked at (from the other side of the glass), with one eye, close to, for almost an hour

Hans Arp—Collage with Squares Arranged According to the Laws of Chance

Surrealism (c. 1924 - 1966)

Art based on dreams, the unconscious, and fantasy; paintings characterized by the juxtaposition of seemingly irrelevant and unrelated images often realistically reproduced, but placed in unexpected situations.

Max Ernst–Swamp Angel
Salvador Dali–Mae West
Joan Miró–Person Throwing a Stone at a Bird
René Magritte–Man with Newspaper

Abstract Expressionism

A method of painting, rather than a style, which began in the 1940s; images and colors are painted on the canvas in a random and spontaneous way; products of these painters differed–ranged from the drip painting of Pollock to the broad slashing brushstrokes of de Kooning; painters shared a primary interest in the process of applying paint rather than in recognizable subject matter.

Jackson Pollock–One
William de Kooning–Woman and Bicycle
Franz Kline–Painting No. 7
Mark Rothko–No. 10

Pop Art

A movement that originated in the United States during the late 1950s; the everyday environment of Americans–comic books, advertisements, and mass-produced products–provided the subject matter for Pop artists.

George Segal–Cinema
Jasper Johns–Three Flags
Claes Oldenburg–Soft Scissors
Robert Rauschenberg–Hot Dog
Andy Warhol–Coca Cola Bottles

Op Art

A movement in abstract art that developed in the United States around 1960, at about the same time as Pop but in a different direction; characterized by optical illusions and impressions of movement.

Joseph Albers–Fugue
Bridget Riley–White Disks II
Victor Vasarely–Vega
Richard Anuskiewicz–Entrance to Green

Minimal Art

This art lacks personal involvement and tactile qualities of the works of the Abstract Expressionists; work characterized by smooth surfaces, pure color, simple geometric forms, and mechanical precision.

Ellsworth Kelly–Red Blue Green
Frank Stella–Empress of India
Kenneth Noland–Via Blues

ART FORMS

The following common art forms and media are often part of a classroom art program. The examples of works for use in children's art experiences are usually obtainable from art books, postcards, and inexpensive prints.

Sculpture

Alexander Archipenko–Woman Combing Her Hair
Umberto Boccioni–Unique Forms of Continuity in Space
Michelangelo Buonaratti–La Pietà
Alberto Giacometti–Man Pointing
Aristide Maillol–Mediterranean
Henry Moore–Reclining Figure
Rodin–The Burghers of Calais

Mosaics

Marc Chagall–Knesset, Jerusalem

Tapestries

Marc Chagall–Knesset, Jerusalem

Murals

Marc Chagall–Lincoln Art Center, New York
Jose Clemente Orozco–Catharsis, Palace of Fine Arts, Mexico City
Diego Rivera–Stairway in the National Palace, Mexico City
David Alfaro Siqueiros–Elements, National Preparatory School, Mexico City

Stained Glass

Marc Chagall–U.N. Building, New York; Hadassah Synogogue, Jerusalem

Paper Cutouts

Henri Matisse–Parakeet and Siren

Collage

Georges Braque–Bach
Pablo Picasso–Guitar
Kurt Schwitters–Disjointed Forces

Pastel

Mary Cassatt–Mother Feeding a Child
Jean Chardin–Self Portrait with Spectacles
Edgar Degas–The Tub
Quentin Latour–Mademoiselle Fel

Woodblock Printing

Albrecht Dürer–The Four Horsemen of the Apocalypse
Paul Gauguin–Offerings of Gratitude
Japanese and Chinese Woodblock Prints

Use of Line

Albrecht Dürer–All woodcuts
Jean Ingres–The Guillon–Lethière Family

Mobiles

Alexander Calder–Heads and Tails

Watercolor

John Sell Cotman–Greta Bridge
Alexander Cozens–View from Mirabella
Winslow Homer–Sloop Bermuda
John Marin–The Singer Building
Andrew Wyeth–Delphinium

ART VOCABULARY

armature–Skeletonlike framework upon which any type of media can be hung or modeled.

Art Nouveau–A widespread movement in architecture and design that spanned from the second half of the 19th century to the outbreak of World War I. Two major styles appear within Art Nouveau–one characterized by curving, twisting lines and asymmetry, as in the works of Aubrey Beardsley, Louis Comfort Tiffany, and Antoni Gaudi; the other by severe geometry and reductive ornamentation exemplified by Charles Rennie Mackintosh and J.M. Olbrich.

bas-relief (low relief)–Sculpture carved so as to project from a flat background as on a coin.

Bauhaus–School of design founded by Walter Gropius in Germany in 1919, closed by Hitler; combined all the arts, from applied arts to fine arts, with the materials and techniques of modern technology.

brayer–A rubber roller used for inking printing blocks.

broken color–Application of short strokes or small dabs of paint beside each other, which viewed from a distance blend together to form a new color.

calligraphy–Beautiful or decorative handwriting; a design created by the arrangement of letters to form a pattern.

caricature–A drawing that exaggerates the features of a person.

cartoon—A full-scale drawing on paper from which a painting, especially murals, are made. Also designates humorous drawings such as comic strips, caricatures, or political satires.

chiaroscuro—An Italian word meaning light and dark. Refers to the manner in which a painter handles atmospheric effects by use of values, tones, or light and dark shading.

chroma—The intensity or purity of a color.

collage—A composition made by pasting scraps of various material such as newspaper, wallpaper, photographs, and fabric on a flat surface.

cloisonné (cloy-zoh-nay′)—An enameling process in which cells made of metal strips or wire are filled with colored enamels and baked or fired in a kiln.

complementary colors—Colors that are opposite each other on a color wheel, such as red and green; when mixed together the original intensities are grayed or neutralized.

contour—The line bounding a figure or object, creating an illusion of mass; outline.

crosshatch—A shading made by two sets of parallel lines crossing over each other, most often used in drawing and printing.

facade—Usually the front of a building.

fixative—A transparent varnish which is sprayed on pencil, chalk, or charcoal drawings to prevent smudging.

foreshortening—A method of reducing, often with distortion, parts of an object not parallel to the picture plane in order to convey depth and dimension.

fresco—Italian word for fresh. The technique of painting on wet plaster with pigments mixed with water. Paint is absorbed by the plaster and becomes chemically bound to it. Dry fresco (fresco secco) uses the same paint on dry plaster. Can also mean painting done in either manner.

frottage—A reproduction of a relief surface made by covering it with paper and rubbing it with pencil, pastel, crayon, etc. Also called a rubbing.

genre painting—A work that depicts a scene from everyday life.

gesso (jess′-oh)—A mixture of plaster and glue, or gypsum, used to prepare a surface for painting.

gouache (goo-ahsh′)—An opaque watercolor made by adding white to a transparent watercolor.

hue—The name of a color—red, blue, etc.

impasto—Paint applied thickly by a brush or knife.

kinetic art—All art forms in which movement appears to take place or actually does take place, often induced by the effect of light. See works by Abraham Palatnik, Nicolas Schöffer, and Victor Vasarely.

line—An invention of man used to delineate the contour of an object and to define space.

lithography—Printmaking process in which a design is drawn onto a polished stone or metal plate with an oily crayon or other greasy material. After moistening the entire surface, ink is applied which adheres only to the lines drawn.

mass—Shapes or forms; volume or area, as opposed to space.

monochromatic color—The different values or intensities of one color.

mosaic—Designs or pictures made by setting small pices of material—glass, marble, or stones—in concrete or plaster, on surfaces such as walls or floors.

montage—A composition made by fitting together pictures or parts of pictures. In motion pictures, it refers to a rapid sequence of images or pictures.

mural—A large painting done directly on a wall or done separately and affixed to a wall.

negative space—The space around objects or shapes.

opaque—Nontransparent.

palette—A thin board or tablet on which colors are placed and mixed. Also refers to the colors used by an artist or group of artists.

pastel—Ground pigments compressed into a chalklike stick. Also, work done in this medium.

pointillism—A painting technique in which a series of small dots of pure color are systematically placed next to each other; also referred to as Divisionism.

primary colors—The three basic colors from which most other colors are made: red, yellow, and blue.

rhythm—The recurrence or repetition of features or objects in a work of art.

secondary colors—Colors containing equal amounts of two primary colors: orange, violet, and green.

sgraffito—A design made by scratching through a surface layer such as glaze or plaster to reveal a different-colored surface beneath.

shade—A darker value of a color, obtained by mixing black to the hue.

shape—The contours of a form of an object.

symmetry—A balance achieved by the arrangement of forms on both sides of an imaginary axis.

terra cotta—An Italian word for cooked-earth. Reddish brown clay used for pottery, sculpture, or building material.

tertiary colors—Colors produced by mixing a primary with a secondary hue: red-orange, blue-green, yellow-green.

tesserae—Small pieces of glass or stone used in making mosaics.

texture—The surface of a work of art—rough, smooth, shiny.

tint—A light value achieved by adding white to a hue.

trompe-l'oeil (trohmp-loy′)—French word for "deceive the eye"; a type of painting in which the objects depicted appear to be real.

triptych—A three-paneled picture, carving, or work of art.

value—The lightness or darkness of a color.

vanishing point—The point on the horizon toward which parallel lines appear to converge.

wash—A thin, transparent film of color, usually watercolor or ink.

COLOR WORDS

Reds

carmine
cerise
cherry
coral
crimson
damask
pink
rose
ruby
salmon
scarlet
titian
vermillion

Browns

beige
bronze
chocolate
cinnamon
coffee
ecru
fawn
hazel
henna
khaki
mahogany
puce
sienna
tan
taupe
tawny
umber

Yellows

amber
buff
canary
champagne
eggshell
gold
lemon
ocher
saffron
xanthic

Purples

fuchsia
heliotrope
lavender
lilac
magenta
maroon
mauve
plum
violet

Whites

alabaster
cream
ivory
pearl

Oranges

apricot
copper
peach
rust
tangerine

Greens

chartreuse
emerald
lime
reseda

Blues

aquamarine
azure
bice
cerulean
indigo
sapphire
turquoise

Blacks

ebony
raven
sable
silver
slate

Color Word Activities

1. Arrange the hues in each color group from light to dark by making a list, painting samples of the colors, or attaching to a sheet of paper samples from fabric, thread, magazines, clothing catalogs, paint chip samples, or nature.

2. Make lists of color words that describe colors by naming objects. These objects can either be added as adjectives or be the names of the colors themselves.

   pea green periwinkle blue avocado green fire engine red
   salmon peach fawn

3. List colors that could fit into more than one major color category.

   rust—Is it brown or orange? coral—Is it red or orange?
   puce—Is it red or brown? chartreuse—Is it yellow or green?

4. Experiment with paint to develop formulas for various hues.

   1 part yellow + 2 parts orange = ______________________________

   Measure parts by a teaspoon, drops from a straw, or a medicine dropper.

5. Describe colors using words.

   chartreuse—a bright greenish-yellow
   reseda—a dull grayish-green
   slate—dark grayish-blue

6. Use paint catalogues or color charts to find and list color names. See which of these are not in the dictionary. Tell which of these words you think may someday enter the dictionary due to common use in everyday language.

MUSICAL PERIODS

Pre-17th Century

Characterized by the development of instruments, notation system, major diatonic scale, and five-lined staff.

Orlando Di Lasso—the height of Renaissance music, religious as well as Italian madrigals and chansons

Giovanni Pierluigi di Palestrina—prominent at the height of Renaissance music; one of the greatest composers of church music—Missa Papae Marcelli (Marcellus Mass)

17th Century

This was a period of great musical progress; generally thought of as the beginning of modern music.

Baroque Period: late 1500s to middle 1700s

Began with a rebellion against the polyphony of Renaissance music, except in the form of counterpoint; grand and brilliant music; rich display of color with contrasting effects between slow and fast, solo and chorus, loud and soft; masses of ornamentation, sometimes excessively exaggerated; elaborate harmonics; often massive effects of voices and instruments; attempted a display of virtuosity.

Johann Sebastian Bach—called the father of modern music

- Magnificat (organ music)
- Brandenburg Concertos
- Prelude and Fugue in D Major
- Fantasia and Fugue in G Minor
- St. Matthew Passion (cantata)
- B Minor Mass
- The Well-Tempered Clavier

George Frederick Handel

- Fireworks Music
- The Beggar's Opera
- The Messiah (oratorio)

Jean-Baptiste Lully—founder of French opera

- Le Bourgeois Gentilhomme—The Middle-Class Nobleman—composed with Molière
- Alceste (opera)

Claudio Monteverdi—a bridge between Renaissance and the Baroque
- Orfeo (opera)
- Hear the Murmuring Waters (from Book II of madrigals)

Henry Purcell—England's greatest composer
- "Dido's Lament" from Dido and Aeneas (opera)
- Golden Sonata in F

Alessandro Scarlatti
- Il Tigrane (opera)
- Il Trionfo del l'onore—The Triumph of Honor (comic opera)

Domenico Scarlatti—remembered for harpsichord compositions; called the father of modern keyboard technique
- Sonate Pastorale

"Rococo" Period: the last thirty to forty years of the Baroque period

A transition period into the Classical; light, highly ornamented style.

Karl Philipp Emanuel Bach
- Solfeggietto

Antonio Vivaldi
- The Seasons, Op. 8 (Le quattro stagione)
- La Stravaganza, Op. 4 (twelve concertos)

Classical Period: middle 1700s to early 1800s

Reflected the ideal of an impersonal, natural concept of beauty; displayed definite patterns with strict adherence to structure and balance; elegant, formal and restrained; significant instrumental development (clarinet, trumpet, hunting horn, piano)

Luigi Boccherini
- Minuet from String Quartet, Op. 13, No. 4

Muzio Clementi
- Gradus ad Parnassum—Steps to Parnassus, 100 piano études, still used by many piano students

Christopher Willibald Gluck
- Orfeo ed Euridice
- Alceste
- Don Juan (ballet)

Joseph Haydn
- London Symphonies
- Toy Symphony
- The Creation (oratorio)

The Seasons (oratorio)
Farewell Symphony

Wolfgang Amadeus Mozart
The Marriage of Figaro (opera)
Don Giovanni (opera)
The "Jupiter" Symphony (Symphony #41 in C Major)

Ludwig Van Beethoven–Often called the bridge between the Classical and Romantic periods; a pioneer figure whose compositions bear characteristics of both periods, yet were uniquely individual; demonstrated that music could reveal the composer's character and be more than impersonal and stylized in definite patterns; brought the symphony to its most perfect stage of development; perhaps the most outstanding composer of western music.

Eroica (Third Symphony)
Fifth Symphony, in C Minor
Pastoral (Sixth Symphony)
Ninth Symphony (contains a choral finale)
Emperor Concerto (#5 in Eb major, op. 73)
Pathétique Sonata
Moonlight Sonata
Fidelio (Beethoven's only opera)
Violin Concerto

Romantic Period: early 1800s to late 1800s

Characterized by music freed of rigid structures; expressed emotion and revealed composers' individuality; often used to tell a story and portray events and scenes; music began to be identified with the country of the composer.

(Italy) *Giacomo Puccini*
La Bohème (opera)
Tosca (opera)
Madame Butterfly (opera)

Gioacchino Rossini
William Tell (opera)
The Barber of Seville (opera)
Peteti Messe solunnelle (Short Solemn Mass)

Giuseppe Verdi
Aïda (opera)
La Traviata (opera)

(Germany-Austria) *Johannes Brahms*
- A German Requiem
- First Symphony
- Variations on a Theme by Haydn

Felix Mendelssohn
- Midsummer's Night Dream
- Hebrides Overture (Fingal's Cave)
- "Spring Song"–No. 30 from Songs Without Words (collection of piano pieces)

Franz Schubert–famous as greatest composer of "lieder," German art-songs
- Gretchen at the Spinning Wheel
- The Erl-King
- Unfinished Symphony
- Rosamunde Music
- C Major Symphony (The Great)

Robert Schumann
- Piano Concerto in A Minor
- Humoresque
- Abegg Variations

Johann Strauss (the Younger)
- Die Fledermaus (opera)
- Tales from the Vienna Woods

Richard Wagner
- Tristan and Isolde (opera)
- Tannhäuser (opera)
- The Ring of the Nibelung (opera)

(France) *Hector Berlioz*
- Roman Carnival Overture
- Fantastic Symphony
- The Childhood of Christ (oratorio)
- "Rákóczi March" from The Damnation of Faust

Georges Bizet
- Carmen (opera)
- Children's Games (pieces for piano duet)

Camille Saint-Saëns
- The Carnival of the Animals
- Danse macabre (Dance of Death)
- Cello Concerto No. 1

(Hungary) *Franz Liszt*
- Hungarian Rhapsodies
- Mephisto Waltz
- Prometheus (symphonic poem)

(Poland) *Frédéric Chopin*
- Minute Waltz (Waltz in Db, Op. 64, No. 1)
- Military Polonaise (Polonaise in A, Op. 40, No. 1)
- Prelude in A, Op. 28, No. 7
- Prelude in C Minor, Op. 28, No. 20

(Bohemia) *Anton Dvořák*
- New World Symphony
- Slavonic Rhapsodies

Bedřich Smetana
- My Country (six symphonic tone poems)
- From My Life (string quartet)

(Russia) *Modest Moussorgsky*
- Boris Godunov (opera)
- Songs and Dances of Death

Nikolai Rimsky-Korsakov
- Scheherazade (symphonic suite)
- The Russian Easter Overture

Piotr (Peter) Ilyich Tchaikovsky
- The Nutcracker Suite (ballet)
- Swan Lake (ballet)
- Sleeping Beauty (ballet)
- 1812 Overture
- Pathétique Symphony
- Romeo and Juliet (overture-fantasy)
- First Piano Concerto

(Norway) *Edvard Grieg*
- Peer Gynt Suite

(United States) *Edward MacDowell*
- Indian Suite
- Woodland Sketches
- The Tragica Sonata

John Philip Sousa
- Semper Fidelis
- The Washington Post March

Modern Period: late 1800s to middle 1900s

This was music generally written to escape the romantic tradition, the expected, and the commonplace: neoclassicism—an attempt to apply the modern concepts of rhythm and tonality to the classic forms; impressionism—expression of the reaction of the senses to nature, events, and emotions; beauty of tone, rich use of color, whole-tone scale, and new harmonic devices; often programmatic, intended to transmit specific meaning to the listener; experimentalism—music involving atonality, bitonality, tone clusters, and other experimental concepts; some use of electronic instruments

Béla Bartók
- String quartets
- Mikrokosmos (children's piano pieces)

Claude Debussy
- The Afternoon of a Faun
- "Iberia" from Images
- Children's Corner

George Gershwin
- Rhapsody in Blue
- An American in Paris (symphonic poem)
- Piano Concerto in F

Paul Hindemith
- Suite 1922
- When Lilacs Last in the Dooryard Bloom'd (based on a poem by Walt Whitman)

Charles Ives
- Concord Sonata
- Three Places in New England
- A Symphony: Holidays

Sergei Prokofiev
- Classical Symphony
- Peter and the Wolf
- Alexander Nevsky (cantata)
- Scythian Suite

Maurice Ravel
- Spanish Rhapsody
- Daphnis and Chloe (ballet)
- Fountains (Jeux d'eau)

Arnold Schoenberg
- Five Orchestral Pieces, Op. 23
- A Survivor of Warsaw
- Pierrot Lunaire (Pierrot by Moonlight)

Richard Strauss
Der Rosenkavalier (opera)
Aus Italien (From Italy)

Igor Stravinsky
Petrushka (ballet)
The Firebird (ballet)
Symphony of Psalms
The Rite of Spring (ballet)
Ragtime for Eleven Instruments (jazz)

Contemporary Period: middle 1900s to present

Characterized by continuing experimentalism; some attempts to reconcile neoclassicism with some experimentalist ideas; new and exciting uses of instruments, fresh tone qualities and structures.

Benjamin Britten
The Young Person's Guide to the Orchestra
Peter Grimes (opera)
Spring Symphony

Aaron Copland
Rodeo (ballet)
Billy the Kid (ballet)
Appalachian Spring (ballet)

Dmitri Shostakovich
Symphony No. 1
The Nose (opera)
Katerina Ismailova (opera)

Karl-Heinz Stockhausen—one of the pioneers of electronic music
Zeitmasse (Measures of Time)
Momente (Moments)
Microphonie I

Heitor Villa-Lobos
Bachiana brazileiras, No. 5
Chôros

MUSICAL FORMS

This list of musical forms is grouped according to the general period of their development or perfection. A suggested example for listening follows each form.

Middle Ages: religious music

chants (plainsongs)–single melodic lines sung by a group; later became polyphonic (two or more melodies woven together)

Gregorian chants, Ambrosian chants

Middle Ages: secular music

folk music
canons (rounds) of the minstrels and troubadours
Summer Is Icumen In (one of the earliest canons, 13th century)

Renaissance

madrigal–in the 14th century, a poem set to music in two voice-parts; by the 16th century, often very fine, free-form poetry, still in counterpoint, although later developing into more chordal forms; eventually developing into one-, two-, three-, and four-part cantatas

Now Is the Month of Maying, Thomas Morley

The Swan Song, Orlando Gibbons

motet–vocal music sung by a group, usually two-part, without orchestral accompaniment, in strict rhythm; later, more parts were added until, by the mid-16th century, the motet became the sacred counterpart of the madrigal

Motets by Palestrina and J.S. Bach

Baroque Period: musical forms

chorale prelude–music based on a chorale melody, composed for the organ

Three Chorales for Organ, César Franck (examples of chorale preludes, although not of the Baroque Period)

concerto grosso–a sonata for several solo instruments (often two violins and a cello) alternating with full orchestra

Brandenburg Concertos, J.S. Bach

dance suite (partita)–short, contrasting dance movements; four usual movements were the allemande, courante, saraband, and gigue

J.S. Bach wrote six French suites, six English suites, and six partitas

fugue–a melody carried on in several overlapping voices

The Art of the Fugue, J.S. Bach

passacaglia (chaconne)–slow and stately dance suite, usually in triple meter

Passacaglia in C Minor, J.S. Bach

rondo–music with a theme that recurs in its original key at certain intervals; later, often used as last movements in compositions by Haydn, Mozart, Beethoven

Last movement of Piano Sonata in A, K. 331, Wolfgang Amadeus Mozart

toccata–keyboard composition with elaborate and rapid passage work, such as runs and arpeggios

Toccata and Fugue in D Minor, J.S. Bach

Toccatas, Girolamo Frescobaldi

trio sonata–in this early development, the sonata was music of a single two- or three-part movement, usually with three voice-parts performed by four instruments

Golden Sonata in F, Henry Purcell

Baroque Period: vocal forms

cantata–short version of the oratorio, usually written on secular themes

Suddenly, Shall the Day Appear, Paul Hindemith

Cantata No. 140–Wachet Auf, J.S. Bach

chorale–a simple hymn, enlarged and ornamented for instruments; later expanded and used in church cantatas

A Mighty Fortress Is Our God, Martin Luther

grand opera–generally applied to early Italian operas and later works with involved, serious plots; also, today applied to operas with lavish productions

Aïda, Giuseppe Verdi (example of grande opera, although not of the Baroque Period)

opera–a drama performed by singing, with costumes, scenery, action, and orchestral accompaniment (some later operas employed ballet groups, also)

Carmen, Georges Bizet (example of opera, although not of the Baroque Period)

oratorio–of religious nature, usually with scriptural text; tells a story; for voices with orchestral accompaniment; usually no action, scenery, or costumes

The Messiah, George Frederick Handel

Classical Period

concerto–sonata for solo instrument with orchestral accompaniment, usually of the following three movements: (1) sonata form, (2) movement in a slower tempo, (3) lively rondo, theme with variations, or again, a movement in sonata form

Concerto No. 1 in Bb Minor, Peter Ilyich Tchaikovsky

chamber music–sonata written for instrumental groupings, such as the string quartet or woodwind quintet, to be performed in a small place

Trout Quintet, Franz Schubert

sonata–developed into a major composition for solo instrument (occasionally two or three may be used) of the following four sections: (1) the allegro, fast movement, (2) a slow movement, (3) a minuet or scherzo, sometimes omitted, (4) a finale, usually fast

Pathètique Sonata, Ludwig van Beethoven

sonata-allegro form–a significant development of the period, used as the first movement of sonatas, symphonies, overtures, and chamber works, with the following sections: (1) statement of a theme, (2) development of theme at length, (3) restatement of original theme

First movement from Sonata, Op. 2, No. 1, Beethoven

symphony–sonata for full symphony orchestra; nearly every major composer wrote at least one symphony

Symphony No. 8 in B Minor (Unfinished), Franz Schubert

Romantic Period

art songs ("lieder")–songs with music composed to fit the text of romantic poetry, often without repetition of stanzas and refrains as in folk songs

Mullerlieder and *Gretchen Am Spinnrade,* Franz Schubert

ballet–a story told in dancing; music written for ballet is frequently used in concerts

Giselle, Adolphe Adam

comic opera (sometimes called operetta and light opera)–lighter, less serious, usually shorter version of the opera form; usually includes speaking roles

The Student Prince, Sigmund Romberg

concert overture–resembles the overture to an opera but is meant to be played in a concert hall as an independent composition

Academic Festival Overture, Johannes Brahms

music-dramas–Richard Wagner's strong, cyclical operas demanding more staging, vocal stamina, and physical endurance than earlier operas

Tristan and Isolde, Richard Wagner

symphonic poem (called tone poem in the Modern Period)—a single symphonic picture, without separate movements, in which the music usually follows a story

Romeo and Juliet (symphonic poem)—Peter Ilyich Tchaikovsky

Don Quixote (tone poem)—Richard Strauss

symphonic suite (program symphony)—lighter version of the symphony, consisting of sections that are related through a chain of events or story

Scheherazade, Nicolai Rimsky-Korsakov

Some Other Forms

aleatory music—music incorporating the element of chance; not all the pitches or rhythms are specified; performers may introduce random elements; no two performances are alike
Stockhausen, Cage (composers)

étude—an instrumental composition designed to help improve the player's techniques
Revolutionary Étude, Chopin

fantasia—a work in free form, according to the composer's desires, not following a strict scheme, although often versions of more standard forms
Wanderer Fantasie in C, Schubert

free form—may not follow any conventional succession of themes; composer then works for unity with harmonization and orchestration
Jeux (Games), Debussy

march—music with a strong rhythm and regular phrases, usually in 2/4 or 4/4 time, suitable for accompanying a marching group
John Philip Sousa's marches

overture—a composition that introduces a longer work, such as an opera or oratorio
Overture on Hebrew Themes, Prokofiev

rhapsody—a free form, relatively short composition, expressing a particular mood
Rhapsody on a Theme by Paganini, Rachmaninoff

scherzo—a movement from a sonata, usually involving an element of surprise; or an independent piece of music that is serious and dramatic rather than playful
Chopin, Brahms

serenade—an instrumental composition for a small group of instruments, usually consisting of several movements
A Little Night Music, Mozart

theme and variations—a series of different treatments of a theme, with key changes, altered rhythm and tempo, or other elements for some of the variations
Variations on a Theme by Handel, Brahms

MUSIC VOCABULARY

a cappella—singing without instrumental accompaniment

accent—an emphasis that makes one note of a measure sound more important than others

arpeggio—a series of chord tones, played in quick succession

bar—*see* measure

chord—tones sounded together; usually refers to three or more tones

coda—a concluding section added after the main piece is finished

counterpoint—combination of two or more melodies, played together, but retaining each one's identity

downbeat—the first accented beat in a measure

dynamics—the contrasts and progressions between the loudness and softness of the music (*see* Dynamics Marks, page 208)

embellishment—*see* ornament

expression—the feeling or mood to be conveyed by the music; expression marks, added by the composer, give the performer detailed directions on how to play (*see* Expression Marks, page 207)

fifth—an interval of five steps between tones; fifth note of a scale

form—the structure of the musical composition

glissando—a "slide"; moving rapidly up or down the scale by sliding a finger along a string, on stringed instruments, or keys, on a piano

harmonics—faint, flutelike sounds of string instruments produced by lightly touching a string, rather than pressing firmly

harmony—the combining of tones; the study of chord combinations and progressions

homophony—a single melody, with its accompanying chords and harmony

improvise—to make up melodies and harmonies while singing or playing, without a preconceived plan

incidental music—music added to a play or film to set a mood or add excitement

interval—the difference (distance) between the pitch of two sounds

key—the "home" center of a musical work; the scale or series of tones whose center (point of rest) is the key name

libretto—the text of the words to be sung in an opera, oratorio, or musical play

measure (bar)—a unit of time in music with a given number of beats

melody—a succession of notes with a definite pattern

ornament (embellishment)–decorations of the melody (grace notes, trills, etc.)

pitch–sound of a musical tone, either high or low; relation of one tone to another

polyphony–*see* counterpoint

rhythm–the arrangement in music of accented and unaccented, long and short, sounds

scale–a series of tones leading from one tone to its octave; the most common scales are major, minor, chromatic, and whole tone

staff–the lines and spaces on which notes are written

syncopation–a shifting of the accent (usually on the first beat of a measure) to one of the weaker beats in the measure

tempo (time)–the rate of speed of the music

third–third note of a scale; an interval of three steps whose tones are written on adjacent lines of adjacent spaces of the staff

timbre (tone color)–quality of tone; the characteristic sound of specific instruments or of the voice

time–*see* tempo

tonality–the quality of belonging to a definite key

tone–a sound with a definite pitch

tone color–*see* timbre

treble–the higher range of sounds

EXPRESSION AND TEMPO MARKS

accelerando (accel.)–becoming quicker (opposite of ritardando)

adagio–slow and leisurely

allegro–quick and cheerful

andante–slowly; gently moving; walking tempo

brillante–bright; sparkling

cantabile–like a singing tone

dolce–sweetly

giocoso–gaily; cheerfully

grave–slow; solemn

largo–very slow; broad; stately

legato–smoothly connected (opposite of staccato)

lento–slowly; between andante and largo

maestoso—majestically
moderato—at a moderate, even pace
presto—very quickly; faster than allegro
risoluto—boldly; resolute
ritardando (ritard.)—becoming slower (opposite of accelerando)
semplice—simply
sostenuto—sustained
staccato—sharp, short notes (opposite of legato)
tranquillo—calm; peaceful
un poco (a poco)—a little
vigoroso—boldly
vivace—quick and lively; faster than allegro
vivo—animated

Some Other Marks

agitato
allargando
allegreto
allegro (molto) brioso
andantino
animato
appassionata
calando
con brio
energico
expressivo
giusto
incalzando
largamente
leggiero
lento doloroso
marcato
morendo
moto
pesante
rigore
ritenuto
rotondo
rubato
sognando
solemne
spirito
subito
tanto
tempestoso

MUSICAL SYMBOLS

Dynamics Marks

very loud *ff*
loud (forte) *f*
fairly loud *mf*
sforzando (play with sudden force) *sf* *sfz*
fairly soft *mp*
soft (piano) *p*
very soft *pp*
crescendo (gradually) getting louder cresc.

decrescendo (gradually) getting softer — decr.

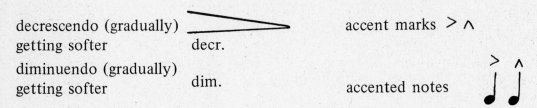

diminuendo (gradually) getting softer — dim.

accent marks > ^

accented notes

Other Musical Symbols

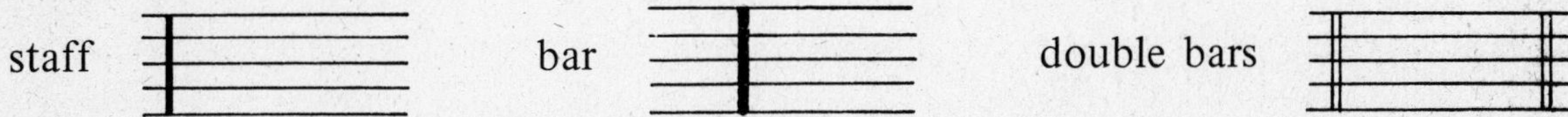

2 3 4 6 9 time (meter) signatures—top number indicates number of beats per measure;
4 4 4 8 8 bottom number indicates the kind of note that receives one beat

$\frac{2}{4}$ = two beats per measure; quarter note receives one beat

common time $\frac{4}{4}$ C

cut time (alla breve); two beats per measure; one beat to each half note ¢

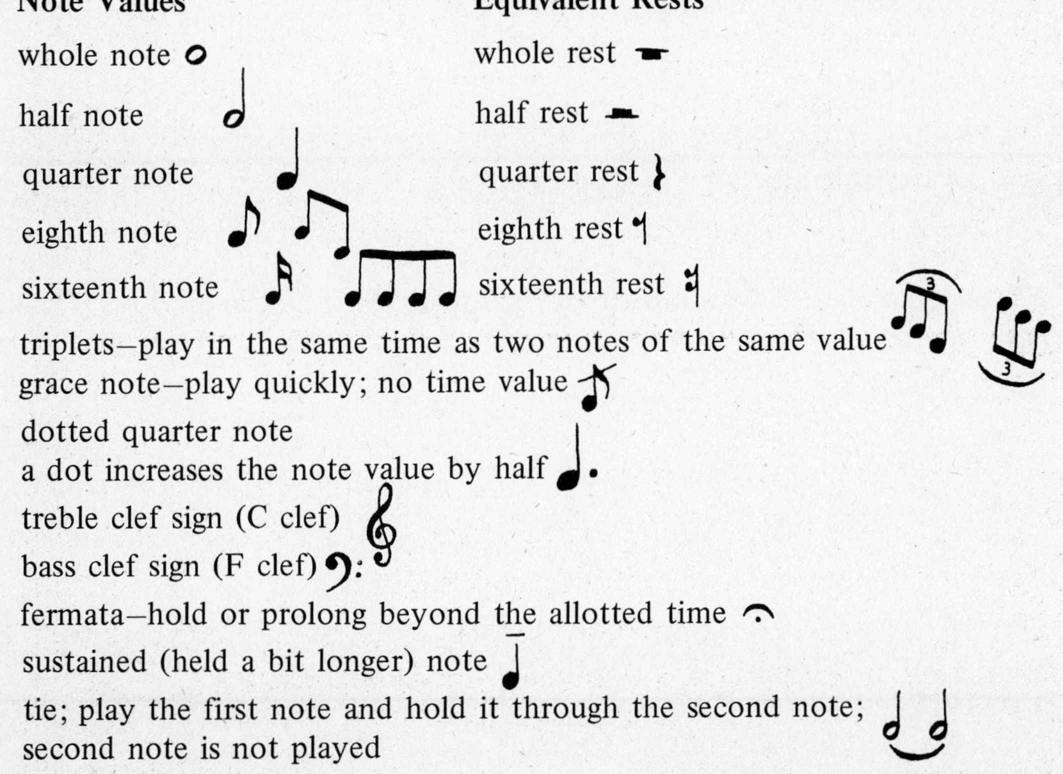

Note Values	**Equivalent Rests**
whole note	whole rest
half note	half rest
quarter note	quarter rest
eighth note	eighth rest
sixteenth note	sixteenth rest

triplets—play in the same time as two notes of the same value

grace note—play quickly; no time value

dotted quarter note
a dot increases the note value by half

treble clef sign (C clef)

bass clef sign (F clef)

fermata—hold or prolong beyond the allotted time

sustained (held a bit longer) note

tie; play the first note and hold it through the second note; second note is not played

staccato note and chord—play in a short, detached way

staccatissimo—very short and detached

phrase—to be played or sung smoothly, to show they belong together in conveying meaning

slur—a phrase to be sung or played very smoothly

trill—rapidly alternating two adjoining notes of the scale tr

flat—lower the note one half step ♭

sharp—raise the note one half step ♯

double flat—lower the note two half steps ♭♭

double sharp—raise the note two half steps

natural—cancel out a given sharp or flat ♮

first ending 1.

second ending 2.

repeat

da capo al fine—return to the beginning of the piece, and play to the word "fine" D.C. al fine

pedal down Ped

pedal up *

up bow V

down bow

arpeggio—play each note of the chord, from low to high, in very rapid succession

MUSIC MAKERS—INSTRUMENTS AND VOICES

The Symphony Orchestra—number of instruments varies, usually 98-112 players

The String Choir (62-66)

Viol Family (bowed or plucked)

- violin 32-34
- viola 12
- violoncello (cello) 10
- double bass 8-10

unbowed strings (2-3)—sometimes placed in a miscellaneous category

- harp 1-2
- piano 1

The Woodwind Choir (16)

All have reeds but the piccolo and flute, which have a hole to blow across

piccolo 1—the highest range in the orchestra

flute 3
oboe* 3
English horn* 1
bassoon* 3
contra bassoon* 1–the lowest range in the orchestra
clarinet 3
bass clarinet 1
saxophone–more recent origin, sometimes used by modern and contemporary composers as a solo instrument

*Have double reeds.

The Brass Choir (13-18)

All have cupped mouthpieces
trumpet 3-5
trombone 3-4
tuba 1
French horn 6-8

The Percussion Group (5-9)

Pitched

tympani (kettledrums) 2-4
xylophone
chimes
glockenspiel (bells)
(xylophone, chimes, glockenspiel: 3-5)

Nonpitched

snare drum	bass drum
gong (tamtam)	triangle
cymbals	tambourine
woodblocks	castanets

Sometimes used with the symphony orchestra: Latin American rhythm instruments such as bongos, marimba, claves, and novelty instruments such as rattles, sandblocks, and sleighbells

Other Instrumental Groupings

Symphonic Band
Chamber Music Groups–string quartets and trios, woodwind quintets, etc.
Chamber Orchestra
Brass Band

Marching Band
Jazz Band
Dance Band
Rock Band
Consort
Broken Consort
Steel Band
Military Band

Some Other Instruments

accordion
bagpipe
balalaika
banjo
baryton
bugle
calliope
chitarrone
chyn (ch'in)
clavichord
clavilux
concertina
crwth
curtal
dulcimer
fife
flageolet
flügelhorn
gittern
glass harmonica
guiro
guitar
gusle
hardanger fiddle
harmonica
harmonium
Hawaiian guitar
helicon
hornpipe
hurdy-gurdy
Irish harp
Jew's harp
kantele
kithara
koto
lur
lute
lyre
mandolin
maracas
marimba
mellophone
monochord
ocarina
oliphant
pandora
pipe
psaltery
qānūn
rabab
racket
rebec
saxhorn
serpent
shakuhachi
shamisen
sitar
spinet
tablas
tambura
theorbo
timbrel
tom-tom
Turkish crescent
'ud
ukulele
vielle
vina
zampogna
zither

Occasionally Used in the Orchestra

basset horn
celesta
cornet
euphonium
harpsichord
heckelphone
oboe do caccia
oboe d'amore
ophicleide
recorder
vibraharp (vibes)

Electronic Instruments

(Instruments fitted with electronic devices, although sound is produced in the usual manner—guitars, flutes, double basses, violins, violas, cellos, saxophones, pianos, harpsichords)

chord organ
combo organ
electronic organ (Hammond organ)
novachord
ondes Martenot
theremin

Instruments at Least 2,000 Years Old That Are Still Played Today

bagpipe
castanets
chyn
finger cymbals
Jew's harp
lyre
panpipes
shawn
sheng
shofar
tambourine
vina

Voice Ranges

Men's voices from low to high:
- bass
- baritone
- tenor

Women's voices from low to high:
- alto (contralto)
  - mezzo-soprano
- soprano

Operatic sopranos:
- coloratura soprano
- dramatic soprano
- lyric soprano

Male soprano parts:
- boy soprano
- falsetto

Bass singers:
- basso buffo
- basso cantante
- basso profondo

Male alto:
- countertenor

Singing Forms and Styles

aria
art song
ballad
barcarole
calypso
carol
chantey (shanty)
folk song
lullaby
popular song
recitative
scatting
song
spiritual
sprechstimme
troubadour
trouvère
yodel

eleven
LITERATURE

GREEK AND ROMAN GODS AND GODDESSES

Greek Name	Roman Name	Role
Zeus	Jupiter ♃	King of the gods
Hera	Juno ⚵	Queen of the gods
Aphrodite	Venus ♀	Goddess of love
Ares	Mars ♂	God of war, wisdom, and crafts
Demeter	Ceres ⚳	Goddess of agriculture
Hades	Pluto ♇	God of the underworld
Hermes	Mercury ☿	Messenger of the gods
Hestia	Vesta ⚶	Goddess of hearth and home
Poseidon	Neptune ♆	God of the sea
Apollo	Apollo	God of sun, music, and medicine
Artemis	Diana	Goddess of the hunt
Asclepius	Aesculapius	God of medicine
Athena	Minerva	Goddess of wisdom
Chloris	Flora	Goddess of flowers
Dionysus	Bacchus	God of wine
Enyo	Bellona	Goddess of war
Eos	Aurora	Goddess of the dawn

Eros	Cupid	God of love
Gaea	Terra	Symbol of the earth
Hebe	Juventas	Goddess of youth and cupbearer to the gods
Hephaestus	Vulcan	God of fire and blacksmith to the gods
Hygeia	Salus	Goddess of health
Hypnos	Somnus	God of sleep
Iris		Goddess of the rainbow
	Janus	God of gates and doors and all beginnings
Morpheus		God of dreams
Nike	Victoria	Goddess of victory
Pan	Faunus	God of flocks, pastures, forests, and wildlife
Panacea		Goddess of healing
Persephone	Proserpina	Queen of the underworld
Rhea		Mother of the gods
Selene	Luna	Goddess of the moon
Thanatos	Mors	God of death
	Nox	Goddess of night

LITERARY AND MYTHOLOGICAL MONSTERS AND CREATURES

Argus–a hundred-eyed giant of Greek mythology

Centaur–Greek mythological monster, half man (from the waist up) and half horse (from the waist down)

Cerberus–a many-headed dog of Greek mythology

Chimera–a fire-breathing monster–part lion, part goat, part dragon–of Greek mythology

Cyclops–a race of one-eyed giants in Greek mythology

Dracula–a centuries-old vampire who was a corpse during the day but came to life at night; from a novel by Bram Stoker

Dragons–monsters famous in legends of many different countries

Frankenstein's monster–a manlike monster created by Dr. Frankenstein in the book of the same name by Mary Wollstonecraft Shelley

Giant–a huge, manlike monster

Gorgons–three female monsters of Greek mythology with serpents for hair

Griffin–a mythical creature, half eagle and half lion

Harpy–a dirty, winged monster with the head of a woman and the tail, legs, and talons of a bird

Hydra–Greek mythological monster; a nine-headed serpent which grew two heads for each one that was cut off

Jabberwock–the fabulous monster in the nonsense poem "Jabberwocky" in *Through the Looking Glass* by Lewis Carroll

Medusa–one of the Gorgons

Minotaur–from Greek mythology; a manlike monster with a bull's head

Pegasus–winged horse of Greek mythology

Phoenix–a legendary Egyptian bird

Roc–a very large, strong legendary bird believed to live in the area around the Indian Ocean

Sphinx–in Greek mythology, a monster with the head of a woman, body and paws of a lion, and huge birdlike wings

Titans–a group of earth giants from Greek mythology, said to have had immense size and brute strength

Unicorn–legendary beast, usually with the head and body of a horse, the hind legs of an antelope, the tail of a lion, and a single, long, sharp twisted horn in the middle of its forehead

Vampires–legendary ghosts which came out of their graves to attack the living

Werewolves–people thought to be transformed into wolves

NEWBERY AWARD WINNERS

The Newbery Medal was named after John Newbery, a famous 18th century seller of children's books. It was first given in 1921, by Frederic G. Melcher, as an incentive for better quality in children's books. The Medal is now donated annually by Daniel Melcher, son of the original donor, to the author of the most distinguished contribution to American literature for children published during the preceding year. Copies of the Newbery list, as well as the Caldecott list that follows, can be given to parents to use as a reference for selecting books from the library, for gifts, or for the home.

1922 *The Story of Mankind.* Hendrik Willem van Loon. (Liveright)
1923 *The Voyages of Doctor Dolittle.* Hugh Lofting. (Lippincott)
1924 *The Dark Frigate.* Charles Hawes. (Little, Brown)
1925 *Tales from Silver Lands.* Charles Finger. (Doubleday)
1926 *Shen of the Sea.* Arthur Bowie Chrisman. (Dutton)
1927 *Smoky, the Cowhorse.* Will James. (Scribner)
1928 *Gayneck, the Story of a Pigeon.* Dhan Gopal Mukerji. (Dutton)
1929 *The Trumpeter of Krakow.* Eric P. Kelly. (Macmillan)
1930 *Hitty, Her First Hundred Years.* Rachael Field. (Macmillan)
1931 *The Cat Who Went to Heaven.* Elizabeth Coatsworth. (Macmillan)
1932 *Waterless Mountain.* Laura Adams Armer. (Longmans Green)
1933 *Young Fu of the Upper Yangtze.* Elizabeth Lewis. (Holt, Rinehart & Winston)
1934 *Invincible Louisa.* Cornelia Meigs. (Little, Brown)
1935 *Dobry.* Monica Shannon. (Viking)
1936 *Caddie Woodlawn.* Carol Brink. (Macmillan)
1937 *Roller Skates.* Ruth Sawyer. (Viking)
1938 *The White Stag.* Kate Seredy. (Viking)
1939 *Thimble Summer.* Elizabeth Enright. (Holt, Rinehart & Winston)
1940 *Daniel Boone.* James Daugherty. (Viking)
1941 *Call It Courage.* Armstrong Sperry. (Macmillan)
1942 *The Matchlock Gun.* Walter D. Edmonds. (Dodd, Mead)
1943 *Adam of the Road.* Elizabeth Janet Gray. (Viking)
1944 *Johnny Tremaine.* Esther Forbes. (Houghton Mifflin)
1945 *Rabbit Hill.* Robert Lawson. (Viking)

1946 *Strawberry Girl.* Lois Lenski. (Lippincott)
1947 *Miss Hickory.* Carolyn Sherwin Bailey. (Viking)
1948 *The Twenty-One Balloons.* William Pene du Bois. (Viking)
1949 *King of the Wind.* Marguerite Henry. (Rand McNally)
1950 *The Door in the Wall.* Marguerite de Angeli. (Doubleday)
1951 *Amos Fortune, Free Man.* Elizabeth Yates. (Aladdin)
1952 *Ginger Pye.* Eleanor Estes. (Harcourt Brace Jovanovich)
1953 *Secret of the Andes.* Ann Nolan Clark. (Viking)
1954 *. . . And Now Miguel.* Joseph Krumgold. (T. Y. Crowell)
1955 *The Wheel on the School.* Meindert De Jong. (Harper & Row)
1956 *Carry On, Mr. Bowditch.* Jean Lee Latham. (Houghton Mifflin)
1957 *Miracles on Maple Hill.* Virginia Sorensen. (Harcourt Brace Jovanovich)
1958 *Rifles for Watie.* Harold Keith. (T. Y. Crowell)
1959 *The Witch of Blackbird Pond.* Elizabeth George Speare. (Houghton Mifflin)
1960 *Onion John.* Joseph Krumgold. (T. Y. Crowell)
1961 *Island of the Blue Dolphins.* Scott O'Dell. (Houghton Mifflin)
1962 *The Bronze Bow.* Elizabeth George Speare. (Houghton Mifflin)
1963 *A Wrinkle in Time.* Madeleine L'Engle. (Farrar, Straus & Giroux)
1964 *It's Like This Cat.* Emily Neville. (Harper & Row)
1965 *Shadow of a Bull.* Maia Wojciechowska. (Atheneum)
1966 *I, Jaun de Pareja.* Elizabeth (Borten) de Trevino. (Farrar, Straus & Giroux)
1967 *Up a Road Slowly.* Irene Hunt. (Follett)
1968 *From the Mixed-Up Files of Mrs. Basil E. Frankweiler.* E. L. Konigsburg. (Atheneum)
1969 *The High King.* Lloyd Alexander. (Holt, Rinehart & Winston)
1970 *Sounder.* William Armstrong. (Harper & Row)
1971 *The Summer of the Swans.* Betsy Byars. (Viking)
1972 *Mrs. Frisby and the Rats of Nimh.* Robert O'Brien. (Atheneum)
1973 *Julie of the Wolves.* Jean Craighead George. (Harper)
1974 *The Slave Dancer.* Paula Fox. (Bradbury)
1975 *M. C. Higgins the Great.* Virginia Hamilton. (Macmillan)
1976 *The Grey King.* Susan Cooper. (Atheneum)
1977 *Roll of Thunder, Hear My Cry.* Mildred D. Taylor. (Dial Press)

CALDECOTT AWARD WINNERS

The first Caldecott Medal, donated by Frederic G. Melcher, was awarded to the artist of the most distinguished American picture book for children published in the United States during the preceding year. The Medal was named for Randolph Caldecott, a famous English illustrator of children's books. The Medal is now donated by Daniel Melcher, son of the original donor.

1938 *Animals of the Bible, a Picture Book.* Illustrated by Dorothy P. Lathrop. Text selected by Helen Dean Fish. (Lippincott)

1939 *Mei Li.* Written and illustrated by Thomas Handforth. (Doubleday)

1940 *Abraham Lincoln.* Written and illustrated by Ingri and Edgar D'Aulaire. (Doubleday)

1941 *They Were Strong and Good.* Written and illustrated by Robert Lawson. (Viking)

1942 *Make Way for Ducklings.* Written and illustrated by Robert McCloskey. (Viking)

1943 *The Little House.* Written and illustrated by Virginia Lee Burton. (Houghton Mifflin)

1944 *Many Moons.* Illustrated by Louis Slobodkin. Written by James Thurber. (Harcourt Brace)

1945 *Prayers for a Child.* Illustrated by Elizabeth Orton Jones. Written by Rachael Field. (Macmillan)

1946 *The Rooster Crows . . .* Illustrated by Maud and Miska Petersham. (Macmillan)

1947 *The Little Island.* Illustrated by Leonard Weisgard. Written by Golden MacDonald. (Doubleday)

1948 *White Snow, Bright Snow.* Illustrated by Roger Duvoisin. Written by Alvin Tresselt. (Lothrop, Lee & Shepard)

1949 *The Big Snow.* Written and illustrated by Berta and Elmer Hader. (Macmillan)

1950 *Song of the Swallows.* Written and illustrated by Leo Politi. (Scribner)

1951 *The Egg Tree.* Written and illustrated by Katherine Milhous. (Scribner)

1952 *Finders Keepers.* Illustrated by Nicolas Mordvinoff. (Harcourt Brace)

1953 *The Biggest Bear.* Written and illustrated by Lynd Ward. (Houghton Mifflin)

1954 *Madeline's Rescue.* Written and illustrated by Ludwig Bemelmans. (Viking)

1955 *Cinderella, or the Little Glass Slipper.* Illustrated and translated from Perrault by Marcia Brown. (Scribner)

1956 *Frog Went A-Courtin'.* Illustrated by Feodor Rojankovsky. (Harcourt Brace Jovanovich)

1957 *A Tree Is Nice.* Illustrated by Marc Simont. Written by Janice May Udry. (Harper & Row)

1958 *Time of Wonder.* Written and illustrated by Robert McCloskey. (Viking)

1959 *Chanticleer and the Fox.* Adapted from Chaucer's *The Canterbury Tales* and illustrated by Barbara Cooney. (T. Y. Crowell)

1960 *Nine Days to Christmas.* Illustrated by Marie Hall Ets. Written by Marie Hall Ets and Aurora Labastida. (Viking)

1961 *Baroushka and the Three Kings.* Illustrated by Nicolas Sidjakov. Written by Ruth Robbins. (Parnassus)

1962 *Once Upon a Mouse.* Retold and illustrated by Marcia Brown. (Scribner)

1963 *The Snowy Day.* Written and illustrated by Ezra Jack Keats. (Viking)

1964 *Where the Wild Things Are.* Written and illustrated by Maurice Sendak. (Harper & Row)

1965 *May I Bring a Friend?* Illustrated by Beni Montresor. Written by Beatrice Schenk de Regniers. (Atheneum)

1966 *Always Room for One More.* Illustrated by Nonny Hogrogian. Written by Sorche Nic Leodhas. (Holt, Rinehart & Winston)

1967 *Sam, Bangs, and Moonshine.* Written and illustrated by Evaline Ness. (Holt, Rinehart & Winston)

1968 *Drummer Hoff.* Written and illustrated by Ed Emberly. (Prentice-Hall)

1969 *The Fool of the World and the Flying Ship.* Written and illustrated by Arthur Ransome. (Farrar, Straus & Giroux)

1970 *Sylvester and the Magic Pebble.* Written and illustrated by William Steig. (Simon & Schuster)

1971 *A Story, a Story.* Written and illustrated by Gail E. Haley. (Atheneum)

1972 *One Fine Day.* Written and illustrated by Nonny Hogrogrian. (Macmillan)

1973 *The Funny Little Woman.* Illustrated by Blair Lent. Written by Arlene Mosel. (Dutton)

1974 *Duffy and the Devil.* Illustrated by Margot Zemach. Retold by Harve Zemach. (Farrar, Straus & Giroux)

1975 *Arrow to the Sun.* Adapted and illustrated by Gerald McDermott. (Viking)

1976 *Why Mosquitoes Buzz in People's Ears.* Illustrated by Leo and Diane Dillon. Written by Verna Aardema. (Dial)

1977 *Ashanti to Zulu.* Illustrated by Leo and Diane Dillon. Written by Margaret Musgrove. (Dial)